T0304896

Cameron Ewen
& Moa Reynolds

SCOTCH

The Balmoral Guide
to Scottish Whisky

MITCHELL
BEAZLEY

First published in Great Britain in 2024 by
Mitchell Beazley, an imprint of
Octopus Publishing Group Ltd
Carmelite House
50 Victoria Embankment
London EC4Y 0DZ
www.octopusbooks.co.uk
www.octopusbooksusa.com

An Hachette UK Company
www.hachette.co.uk

Text and photography pages 13, 14, 15, 40 copyright
© The Balmoral 2024

Design, layout and photography copyright
© Octopus Publishing Group 2024

Distributed in the US by
Hachette Book Group
1290 Avenue of the Americas
4th and 5th Floors
New York, NY 10104

Distributed in Canada by
Canadian Manda Group
664 Annette St.
Toronto, Ontario, Canada M6S 2C8

ISBN 978-1-78472-951-6

A CIP catalogue record for this book is available
from the British Library.

Printed and bound in China.

10 9 8 7 6 5 4 3 2 1

MIX
Paper | Supporting
responsible forestry
FSC® C008047
www.fsc.org

Publisher: Alison Starling
Commissioning Editor: Jeannie Stanley
Editorial Assistant: Ellen Sleath
Art Director: Nicky Collings
Copy-Editor: Laura Gladwin
Picture Research Manager: Giulia Hetherington
Senior Production Controller: Katherine Hockley
Photographer: Perry Graham
Illustrator: Heather Gatley
Book Design: Atwork

All cocktail recipes serve one.

Standard level spoon measurements are used in all recipes.
1 tablespoon = one 15 ml spoon
1 teaspoon = one 5 ml spoon

Both metric and imperial measurements have been given in all recipes. Use one set of measurements only and not a mixture of both.

Eggs should be medium unless otherwise stated. The Department of Health advises that eggs should not be consumed raw. This book contains recipes made with raw eggs. It is prudent for more vulnerable people such as pregnant and nursing mothers, and the elderly to avoid uncooked recipes made with eggs. Once prepared these recipes should be kept refrigerated and used promptly.

Fresh herbs should be used unless otherwise stated. If unavailable use dried herbs as an alternative but halve the quantities stated.

This book includes recipes made with nuts and nut derivatives. It is advisable for customers with known allergic reactions to nuts and nut derivatives to avoid recipes made with nuts and nut oils. It is also prudent to check the labels of pre-prepared ingredients for the possible inclusion of nut derivatives.

Contents

WELCOME TO SCOTCH

Map of Scotland's Whisky

HIGHLANDS

1. Aberfeldy
2. Ardnamurchan
3. Balblair
4. Clynelish
5. Dalwhinnie
6. Deanston
7. Fettercairn
8. Glencadam
9. The GlenDronach
10. Glen Garioch
11. Glenmorangie
12. The Glenturret
13. Royal Brackla
14. Tomatin

SPEYSIDE

15. Aberlour
16. The Balvenie
17. Benriach
18. Benromach
19. Craigellachie
20. Dailuaine
21. GlenAllachie
22. Glenfarclas
23. Glenfiddich
24. The Glenlivet
25. The Glenrothes
26. Glen Grant
27. Glen Moray

28. Longmorn
29. The Macallan
30. Tamdhu

ISLANDS

31. Highland Park
32. Lochranza
33. Tobermory
34. Talisker

ISLAY

35. Ardbeg
36. Bowmore
37. Bruichladdich
38. Bunnahabhain
39. Kilchoman

LOWLANDS

40. Glenkinchie
41. Daftmill
42. Ailsa Bay

CAMPBELTOWN

43. Glen Scotia
44. Glengyle
45. Springbank

BLENDS/GRAIN

46. Cambus
47. Gordon & MacPhail
48. Johnnie Walker

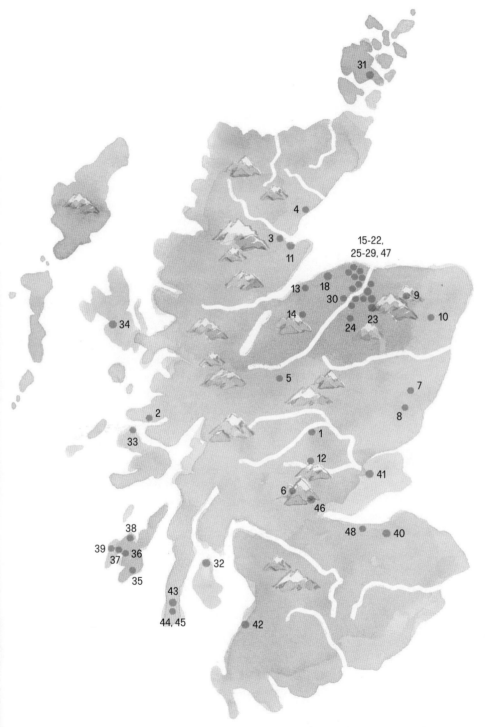

15-22,
25-29, 47

Behind the SCOTCH bar

Stepping inside The Balmoral hotel, located at the very eastern side of Princes Street, Edinburgh, is an invitation to experience its Scottish heritage, brought to life by the colours of the surrounding landscape. Just off to the right of the lobby an intriguing room awaits, with amber walls, brass accents and a slick black marble bar. Immediately your eye is drawn towards the impressive iron cages on one side, which hold over 500 bottles of Scotch whisky from all over Scotland. The comfortable leather armchairs and elegant tartan furnishings make for a perfect spot to sit down and relax with a dram. Welcome to SCOTCH.

This prestigious Edinburgh whisky bar welcomes visitors from all around the world. Some enter through the polished wooden doors as whisky lovers and whisky experts, and others as newcomers eager to embark on their first adventure of sampling the finest dram. With a warming, cosy aura, SCOTCH invites visitors to enter and admire its grand whisky library. All hand-picked by the bar's Whisky Ambassadors, the bottles are prominently displayed so that visitors can browse the collection without the separation of a bar.

As they settle in with their chosen dram and take their very first sip, guests are transported on a journey like no other, through the rolling hills, lochs and fields of Scotland to the individual distilleries where the whiskies are produced, and right back to the comfort of their seat in SCOTCH in the heart of Edinburgh. Equipped with a wealth of knowledge and a love for *uisge beatha* (the Scots Gaelic term for whisky, meaning 'water of life'), SCOTCH's Whisky Ambassadors are ready not only to recommend the perfect dram, but also to tell the story of the whisky and the distillery it originated from. For those looking for a more gentle introduction to the spirit, a range of cocktails are on offer, and delicious nibbles are always on hand, from dark chocolate to smoked almonds.

With this book, the unparalled knowledge and expertise of SCOTCH's Whisky Ambassadors is available for the first time in print. Enjoy flicking through the top 100 whiskies specially selected by SCOTCH's bar manager, and dissect the recommendations and detailed comments on the nose, taste and finish of each

dram. Learn more about the distillery each whisky came from and note the very best way to enjoy it, whether by itself, with water or a mixer of your choice. For whisky lovers searching for the perfect cocktail, there is a special treat just for you. We hope you enjoy your dive into the enchanting world of Scotch whisky and hope to see you very soon at Edinburgh's best-loved whisky bar.

About The Balmoral

The Balmoral hotel is located in the heart of the Scottish capital at 1 Princes Street, Edinburgh's most prestigious address. The building was initially home to the North British Station Hotel, which opened on 15 October 1902 under the ownership of the North British Railway Company. In 1988 the hotel closed for a major refurbishment, reopening three years later under the name that it is known by today: The Balmoral. Six years later, the hotel was bought by Sir Rocco Forte of the Rocco Forte Hotels group, and became the first hotel in his new Rocco Forte Collection.

The building was designed by W Hamilton Beattie and A R Scott, who wanted to incorporate a European style, including details inspired by the French Renaissance and Dutch dormer windows. The Balmoral is an Edinburgh landmark, and to this day its majestic clock tower is an iconic feature of the capital's skyline. Proudly overlooking Princes Street, adjacent to Waverley Train Station, visitors to the city cannot fail to notice it. Famously, the hotel's clock is set to run three minutes fast – a tradition that dates back to the hotel's beginnings, and a helpful encouragement to tardy rail travellers who might be prone to missing their trains.

In September 2013, The Balmoral opened the doors to its whisky bar, aptly named SCOTCH. It offers one of the largest collections of single malt Scotch whiskies in Edinburgh, with over 500 bottles from Speyside, Islay, Campbeltown, the Highlands and the Lowlands. The bar is well looked after by the SCOTCH team of Whisky Ambassadors, who use their wealth of knowledge to guide guests through myriad blends, malts and vintages dating back to 1950.

This book features 100 whiskies hand selected by the SCOTCH team from the bar's prestigious collection. Together they offer a brilliant representation of the diversity and exceptional quality of single malt Scotch whiskies.

How To Taste Whisky

When tasting whisky, most connoisseurs analyse and experience the liquid through five steps: observing the colour, examining the 'legs', nosing the aroma, appreciating the taste and contemplating the finish.

The first and second steps are about the appearance of the whisky. Firstly, what colour does it have? The colour can sometimes indicate how young or old your whisky is – generally, the longer whisky spends in a cask, the darker it gets – as well as the type of cask it was matured in, since the highest-quality whiskies generally only have their natural, cask-derived colour. There are exceptions, of course, as producers are allowed to add a small amount of plain caramel colouring to whisky for consistency between batches. This means that a visual assessment is not always a reliable measure of maturity. A fresh cask, being filled for the first time, is expected to be more 'active' and usually imparts more colour than a refill cask that has been used several times already – but a richer colour does not necessarily mean better or more flavour (see page 26 for more on this).

Secondly, we examine the 'legs'. When the liquid is swirled around in a tasting glass, the alcohol beads around the interior and will drip back down into the bowl. How quickly or slowly do the legs, also called 'tears', run down the sides of the glass? The legs can help indicate if the spirit has an oilier, heavier body (with a slower descent down the glass) or lighter body (quicker descent), which can affect the mouthfeel and texture of the whisky. Different aspects of production help to determine a whisky's body, in particular the shape of the stills. Taller and thinner stills generally produce a lighter style of spirit, as only lighter compounds manage to make it to the top and over to the condensers, whereas shorter stills tend to result in oilier and heavier spirits.

The third step is the nosing, a very significant part of appreciating whisky. If the five steps were to be scaled back to just two, then nosing and tasting would be the most essential. There are different ways of nosing a whisky. Some people like to smell further away from the glass, while some prefer putting their nose close to the spirit, although this can cause a numbing of the nose, or even a bit of a tingle if the

ABV is high. Others swirl the glass from one side to the other to introduce each nostril to the aromas. For those new to whisky, it can be helpful to part the mouth slightly to open up the olfactory system, which usually helps tasters experience less of the alcohol burn and more of the subtle aromas. On the first nosing, it is common to mostly smell the alcohol vapours, which have not yet 'escaped' out of the glass, especially in the first dram of a tasting. It is therefore important to come back to the glass a couple of times to get the nose used to what it is sensing.

The fourth step is what many of us will be most familiar with: the tasting. However, do not throw the whisky to the back of the palate, as people tend to do when they take a shot, otherwise the spirit will not coat the entire palate and the taste buds cannot pick up all the flavours. Instead, allow the whisky to spread out across your tongue and let it coat your entire mouth before swallowing. You will probably notice that some flavours from the nose become more distinct on the palate, while others become harder to detect. You may even identify some characteristics you didn't notice while nosing. Also consider the mouthfeel: is the spirit oily or light? Does it have a ginger- or even wasabi-like heat? All of these indicators tell you something about the whisky and how it was made.

Finally, the finish of a whisky is the flavour and sensation that remains after swallowing the spirit. Different flavours can emerge or intensify here, and a finish can be short or long depending on the length of time the flavour stays on the palate before it disappears. For example, smoky whiskies tend to have a longer finish, as the smoke often has a powerful and lingering impact.

External factors like temperature, ambient aromas, glassware, sounds and even your mood can also impact the flavour of whisky in various ways. It is generally recommended to drink whisky at room temperature, but some prefer to add ice to the glass to cool the whisky down, which tends to make the flavours less intense and more easily identifiable, but it also increases dilution, reduces viscosity and negates any 'burn'. When considering glassware, there are glasses shaped specifically for the enjoyment and appreciation of Scotch whisky, such as the Glencairn glass. The tulip shape is designed to allow drinkers to enjoy fully all aspects of the whisky. It has a wide bowl to allow appreciation of the colour and a tapered opening that captures and focuses the aromas. Another classic glass for whisky is the tumbler or rocks glass, which might not capture the aromas in the same way as a Glencairn, but still offers an enjoyable drinking experience, as it feels comfortable to hold and drink from.

At the beginning of your whisky journey, it is common to struggle with identifying the subtle aromas and flavours described in the distillers' (or reviewers') tasting notes. It can be helpful to try whiskies of various characters – for example, one bourbon matured, one sherry matured and one peated whisky – next to each other to gain a better understanding of how different they can be. Tasting notes will vary from person to person because we all have our own experience of aromas, which depends on our culture, vocabulary and memories. Some people find it easier to describe flavour as colours or shapes rather than in words. Tasting notes can be as simple as a few words, such as apple, vanilla and smoke, or longer sentences, such as 'Walking through an apple orchard on a warm spring afternoon, wearing a perfume with soft and elegant vanilla notes while a cooling breeze brings a whiff of smoke from a nearby bonfire of twigs.' (Turn to page 66 to read the first of SCOTCH's head barman's own tasting notes.)

There are also helpful tools for identifying flavour, such as flavour wheels. Many flavour wheels of varying complexity are available only a short internet search away, but the wheel presented opposite is a simplified version designed to help with describing basic tasting notes. A whisky might be fruity, but what type of fruit would it be? Ripe fruit, cooked fruit, dried fruit? Apples, pears, pineapple or raisins? The flavour wheel takes larger categories, such as fruity and peaty, and suggests words for the flavours you might find in each group to help specify aromas.

Fruity

The fruity category contains flavours that arise during fermentation and distillation. A longer fermentation can result in more fruity and floral aromas, whereas a shorter fermentation can produce a maltier character. Esters are important compounds mainly formed during fermentation. They can be responsible for aromas such as peach, pear, pineapple, banana and apple, although some people experience esters more like acetone rather than fruity.

Cereal

Cereal notes generally come from the barley itself and can be influenced by factors such as how hard the barley is roasted. Barley can be roasted to different levels; common names for these include crystal malt, amber malt and chocolate malt. However, the roasted barley tends to be more frequently used for beer production. The flavours derived from the grain can be concentrated or changed during the production process, for example through mashing and fermentation.

Cask Derived

This category looks at flavours derived from maturation. American white oak (*Quercus alba*) casks usually give notes of vanilla and coconut, on account of the oak's structure and how American casks are generally prepared by US cooperages. Casks made from European oak, *Quercus robur*, or sessile oak, *Quercus petraea*, tend to be spicier and give flavours like cloves. The European species of oak generally contains more tannins than its American cousin. The previous contents of the cask – often bourbon, still wine, sherry or beer – will also impact the flavours and aromas that fall into this category. Oloroso or Pedro Ximénez sherry casks can give the whisky notes of dried fruits and raisins, and red wine cask maturation can result in a character of red berries, for example.

Flavour Wheel

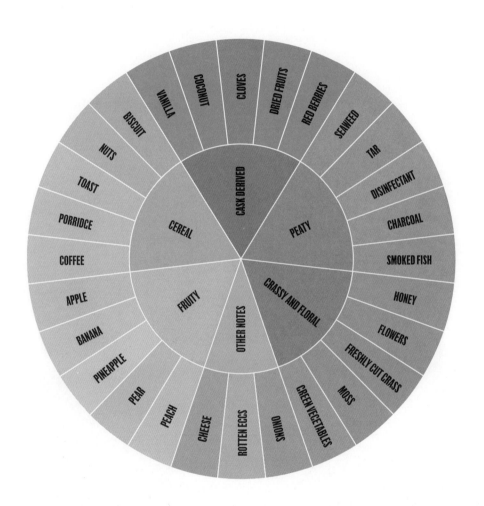

Peaty

Peated characteristics can vary depending on what type of peat has been used to smoke the barley (wet or dry, inland or coastal) and also on the production process (for more on this, see page 38). Nevertheless, all peaty characteristics derive from the peated malt and how much is used in the mash bill (the grain combination). Different cut points (when the spirit is separated) in distillation, shorter or longer fermentation and choice of cask for maturation can all affect how the peat comes across in the finished whisky. Will it be more maritime, with notes of seaweed and tar; medicinal, like disinfectant; fuel-like, with notes of coal, charcoal or petrol; or will it bring more smoky aromas of bonfire, lapsang souchong tea or smoked fish?

Grassy and Floral

Grassy and floral aromas and flavours are also derived primarily from the production stages. Honey is a common tasting note in many Scotch whiskies under the floral umbrella, but whisky can also be floral like a bouquet of flowers or parma violets. On the grassy side, it is not unusual to find aromas like freshly cut grass, moss or green vegetables.

Other Notes

Less desirable aromas, also called off-notes, can also arise during the production of whisky. One of the reasons that copper plays a big part in Scotch whisky production is because it can assist with removing unwanted aromas. Equipment like pot stills and condensers tend to be made out of copper because it affects the character of the whisky by absorbing certain compounds. Sulphur, which occurs naturally during the whisky production process, is often classed as an unwanted characteristic.

These characterics arise during fermentation as well as maturation, and some distilleries run their production to retain some levels of sulphur because it suits their style of spirit, although some notes, like that caused by butyric acid (often described as 'cheesy'), and certain kinds of sulphur (rotten eggs or onions) tend to be undesirable. The aromas that fall under this umbrella are not necessarily bad, however, as some people prefer whiskies that are known for having more of a sulphuric character.

The Top Questions About Scotch Whisky

Scotland's national drink is beloved worldwide and has always been surrounded by a level of mystique. Today, most of the production process has been thoroughly studied so that distillers can perfect their whisky making. However, there is still something magical that happens during maturation that is hard to explain, even for master distillers and top blenders. It is no wonder, therefore, that this fascinating liquid has been surrounded by so many myths over hundreds of years. Although some things cannot be fully explained, many of the most common questions can certainly be answered.

How is whisky made?

Malting
To create the alcohol used in whisky, sugar must be extracted from barley. First the barley is germinated by steeping it in water so that its starches turn into sugars (a process that would occur naturally if it was growing in the fields). Then it is dried using hot air or peat (for a smoky flavour) to halt germination and for the sugar to be extracted before the barley uses it up.

For single malt whisky, the mash bill (the mix of grains used to make whisky) is 100 per cent malted barley.

Milling
The next step is milling the barley into a mixture of flour, husks and grits (different levels of coarseness, where flour is the finest). A balance of coarseness is needed for optimal extraction and to prevent the mixture from clumping and getting stuck in the machinery.

Mashing
Sugar is extracted in the mash tun, a big vessel where the barley mixture is blended with three different batches of water, each increasing in temperature to extract more sugar each time. The sugar dissolves into the water, creating a kind of porridge (oatmeal). Excess water is drained and the liquid (called wort) is moved to the washbacks (tall vessels made out of wood or stainless steel) for fermentation. Leftover solids are separated, dried and often used for animal feed.

Fermentation
In the washbacks, yeast is added to the wort and the mixture is left to ferment for multiple days, varying from 48 to over 100 hours. The yeast 'eats' the sugar, creating by-products of ethanol (alcohol) and CO_2. The liquid, known as wash, is now around 8–10% ABV.

Distillation
The wash is moved into the wash still for its first distillation (single malt whisky typically has two). The still is heated up to separate the water and the alcohol, concentrating the ABV, which must be at least 40% to qualify as Scotch whisky. The vapours rise up in the still, and once they make it into the lyne arm and across to the condensers, they are cooled down and turned into liquid again. The first part of the run (called foreshots or heads) contains dangerous alcohols like methanol, so the distillers must separate these out into another vessel. The second part (the middle cut or hearts) is the desirable section that is needed for the whisky, but this can also contain leftover solids and other unwanted compounds that must be separated from the middle cut and led into the feints receiver. The foreshots and feints tend to be redistilled to make sure as much as possible has been extracted from them.

The spirit coming off the stills through the middle cut is called low wines and is usually around 20–30% ABV, so is distilled again to concentrate it even further. This time the middle cut spirit ends up around 70% ABV and is known as new make spirit. It needs three years of maturation before it is legally allowed to be called Scotch whisky.

Maturation
Whisky is matured in oak casks of various sizes, many of which have previously held another liquid like bourbon whiskey, sherry or wine. Most distilleries water the new make spirit down to 63.5% before pouring it into the casks.

Following maturation, the contents of the selected casks are usually vatted together, meaning they are blended and left in vessels for their flavours to integrate before they are bottled. Before bottling, the whisky can either be watered down to filling strength or bottled at its natural cask strength.

What is chill-filtering?

There are compounds in whisky that can cause the liquid to turn cloudy in colder temperatures or when water is added. These compounds are created throughout the whisky-making process, especially during fermentation. Some might think that being cloudy means a whisky is faulty, but this is a very natural occurrence. Many whisky brands use a process called chill-filtration, which removes certain compounds so that the whisky's clarity is improved. This is popular with whiskies bottled at 40–46% ABV. The process consists of chilling the whisky down to between 4°C and -10°C (39–14°F) and passing it through a thin filter, which captures and removes heavier compounds such as fatty acids and proteins that can clump together and cause cloudiness in the whisky. These compounds are less likely to clump up and cause haze above 46% ABV. Chill-filtration is therefore considered unnecessary for higher-strength whiskies.

This natural reaction in whisky is not common knowledge, and many brands are worried that hazy whisky would cause consumers to think there was a quality flaw. This led to chill-filtration being introduced and widely adopted by the industry

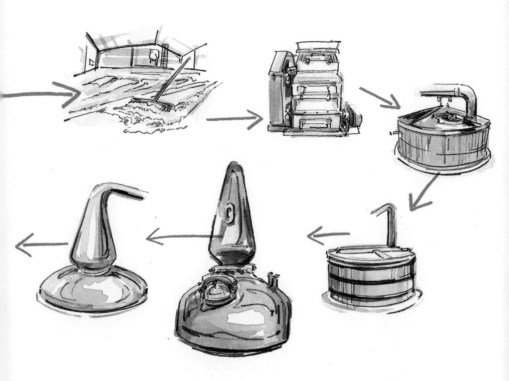

during the 20th century. There is an ongoing debate among whisky drinkers about chill-filtration, however. Some believe it can detract from the flavour and mouthfeel of the liquid, while others believe the effects to be indiscernible. There is also the argument that the esters and fatty acids that disappear during the filtration could affect the flavour. Some say this is for the worse, and some say for the better. Informal studies have been conducted into the discernibility of chill-filtration, but it seems difficult to come to a conclusion. Much as with the addition of caramel colouring, a Scotch whisky distiller does not need to display whether they chill-filter or not on the label. Many brands that do not chill-filter will put the words 'non-chill-filtered' or 'unchill-filtered' on the bottle, and whiskies with lower ABVs are often assumed to have been through filtration.

Although the topic of chill-filtration is occasionally debated, it is important to remember what products support the rest of the industry. The sale and success of chill-filtered and coloured whisky, bottled at 40%, allows brands to also release the exclusive bottles targeted at a different type of consumer.

Does a higher ABV equal more flavour in whisky?

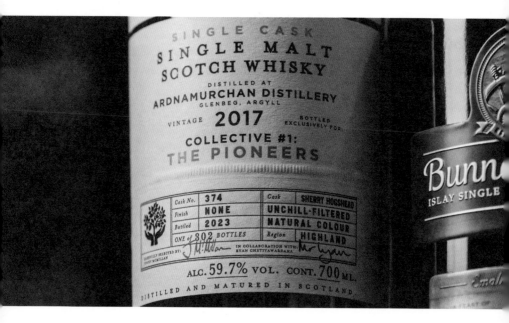

For Scotch whisky, the legal minimum ABV (alcohol by volume) is 40% (80 US proof), but it is not uncommon to see a variety of strengths on different whisky bottles. Some of the most common bottling strengths are 40%, 43% and 46% ABV, but it is entirely up to the distillery what strength they decide upon. Some distilleries bottle their entire core range at the same strength, while others choose different strengths for each bottling.

A higher ABV does not necessarily equal better quality or more flavour, and it can be harder to identify aromas and flavours if the ABV is very high. For higher-

ABV whiskies, it can be a good idea to add a couple drops of water and see if a lower strength can open up lighter or different characteristics in the whisky.

Some bottles will mention the terms 'cask strength' or 'batch strength'. Cask strength indicates that the whisky has been bottled at the same strength it was when it came out of the cask it was matured in, without being diluted to a bottling strength, as whisky often is. The term batch strength is more ambiguous, as it can mean that the whisky has been bottled at the natural strength arrived at when all the casks in the batch were vatted together, or it can be a nominated ABV for that specific batch, chosen by the blender. Either of these can vary between different batch releases. In the relatively cold, humid climate in Scotland, more alcohol will evaporate than water, so the alcoholic strength will decrease over time, which is romantically called the 'angels' share'.

Most, but not all, distilleries water their new make spirit (the liquid that comes off the stills after distillation) down to 63.5% ABV before filling their casks – a strength considered the 'industry standard' for optimal maturation. The number of years the whisky spends in the cask impacts how high (or low) the alcoholic strength will be once it is deemed ready for bottling. This can be a challenge with older whisky, as the alcohol evaporates more quickly than water and decreases in strength with time. As mentioned earlier, the spirit can no longer be bottled as Scotch whisky if it is below 40% ABV, so if the alcohol strength sinks too low, it might need to be blended with other stock to bring it back up.

Many experienced whisky drinkers appreciate a cask-strength whisky because it allows them to add as much or as little water as they would like. Spirits that are sold at set bottling strengths have been positioned at that strength by the master blender, who has deemed it the most favourable strength for the flavours in that expression. They also take into consideration who the intended drinker is, as whisky enthusiasts might not mind higher strengths, while 'entry-level' whiskies tend to be bottled around 40% to be more accessible to a wider audience.

Most distilleries that use double pot still distillation run their spirit to around 70%, and those that use triple distillation can go a bit higher. Double distillation is used by most distilleries in Scotland, since one distillation (the 'wash run') brings the distillate (known as low wines) to around 20% ABV. They need to distil at least one more time to concentrate further the alcohol and reach 40% ABV. However, it is not permitted to distil Scotch whisky to above 94.8% ABV; if this were done, the spirit would instead be classed as a grain-based vodka. The raw spirit is considered neutral above this ABV, and it is a requirement in Scotland that the spirit must taste of its raw material – in the case of single malt, that means barley – to qualify as a whisky.

Is darker whisky better?

Many people believe that the darker in colour a whisky is, the better it will taste, but that is not necessarily true. The colour of a whisky generally derives from the cask, since the new make spirit, fresh from the still, is completely colourless. It is the oak that tends to give the spirit all its glorious colour, which can range from pale straw to rich amber or even dark brown. An older whisky can therefore have a darker colour than a younger whisky from the same cask type. The longer the whisky spends in a cask, the more colour it can absorb.

To make things a little more complicated, the colour the whisky picks up during maturation also depends on the type of cask it has been in. In the Scotch whisky industry today, the most common cask type is the ex-bourbon barrel. These usually hold around 200 litres (53 US gallons), are made from American white oak and have previously held American bourbon whiskey. Since a cask can only be used once for bourbon due to the regulations governing its production, it is perfect for Scotch distilleries to import and repurpose for their own whisky. In Scotland, these ex-bourbon casks are not only used once but two, three and possibly even more times to get the most out of them. This will, of course, affect how much flavour and colour a whisky absorbs from the casks. Think of a cask like a teabag: the first time it is used, the water receives a lot of flavour and colour extraction. On its second use, less flavour and colour stay in the new water. By the third use, the impact is even less. For some whiskies it can be beneficial to use less active casks, such as a second or third fill, especially if the whisky is meant to stay in the cask for a long time. A first-fill cask can give plenty of flavour and colour in a relatively short time, but leaving the liquid for too long can result in a whisky that is overmatured and overly woody, drying or even bitter. The previous contents of the cask also matters: ex-bourbon casks tend to impart that classic golden straw or amber colour that we associate with Scotch whisky. However, an ex-port cask or ex-red wine cask can give the whisky a pink or red hue.

During the whisky-bottling process, Scotch whisky makers are permitted to use a specific type of flavourless and odourless colouring, known as caramel colouring or E150A. This is primarily used to maintain consistency between batches, as there can be a natural variation in colour, even after different casks of single malt have been blended following maturation. If a label states that the whisky has 'natural colour', it does not contain any added colouring, although it is not a requirement in the UK to state on the bottle when colouring has been added. There are some countries where Scotch whisky is sold, like in Germany, where it is a legal requirement to state whether colour has been added on the label. The small quantity needed to maintain batch consistency should not affect the flavour and it is not allowed to exceed the natural range of golden hues that can be derived from the maturation of Scotch whisky in casks. It is important not to alter the colour of Scotch whisky dramatically, as according to Scottish regulations it must retain the colour derived from production.

Does water matter?

Scotland is known for its beautiful, dramatic landscapes full of freshwater lochs and mountain springs. Scottish public drinking water (tap water) has been judged among the highest quality in the world. When it comes to whisky production, water is a fundamental ingredient and resource for the whole process to make the outstanding spirit we know and love. A large quantity of water is needed to make whisky, but only a small proportion of it finds its way into the final drink.

Water is one of three main ingredients for malt whisky, alongside barley and yeast, but it is also used in a variety of ways throughout whisky production. It can be used to cool down equipment such as condensers and, if a distillery is using a steam boiler, it is also used to heat the stills. Water is necessary for cleaning equipment and is often added both before the new make spirit goes into casks for maturation and after maturation to water down the whisky to bottling strength. Because of all of this, a distillery needs to have a clean and reliable water source at all times. Scotland is without doubt a great place for whisky making because of the country's many high-quality water sources. It is, however, debatable whether the water used has any major impact on the flavour of the whisky.

Then there is the question about adding water or ice to a dram of whisky. This will change the character of the whisky, but it can improve the experience. As previously mentioned, water has already been added to create the spirit: it is a necessary component from the start. Most whiskies will have been diluted to bottling strength, commonly 40%, 43% or 46% ABV, decided by the blending team. Many whisky blenders water down their samples quite far below the legal minimum of 40%, as it is their preferred way to analyse the aromas and flavours in the spirit. When adding water to whisky, different compounds disperse differently from others, which means the water can help release certain characteristics at different strengths. When a whisky is bottled at cask strength, it can be even more helpful to add water, as aromas can appear hidden underneath the more powerful alcoholic vapours. Any clean and fresh water, preferably without noticeable mineral or chemical characteristics or too much of an aftertaste, can be added to a glass of whisky.

When adding water to whisky, it is best to start by just adding a drop or two and tasting in between drops. You can always add more, but you cannot take water out of the whisky. Adding ice to a whisky can be a good alternative to adding water. Ice primarily does two things to a spirit: chills and dilutes. Keep in mind that the dilution speed cannot be controlled in the same way it can when adding

a couple of drops of water at a time. Chilling whisky with ice can be a lovely way to enjoy a dram when the weather is hot or if you prefer a less powerful taste, as a colder temperature can make the drinker perceive the alcoholic burn as reduced and the flavours and aromas as slightly muted. Stainless-steel freezer cubes are a great alternative which will cool the whisky without the dilution.

Older vs younger: which is better?

In Scotland, the minimum maturation required to be officially classed as a Scotch whisky is three years in an oak cask. No other wood type is allowed to be used for maturation, but the oak cask has often held another liquid, such as bourbon, sherry or wine, prior to being used for Scotch. There are, of course, many whiskies much older than three years, but there is no optimal age at which the flavours and aromas peak. It is entirely up to the skill and experience of the distillery team to choose when they want to extract the liquid contents of their casks.

There are several factors that explain why people believe that older whisky equals better whisky. Older whisky tends to be more expensive, is sometimes darker in colour (which many also incorrectly equate with more flavour) and often has an increased historical value. One of the reasons older whisky tends to be more expensive is because distilleries do not make a profit from the whisky until it is sold. During this time the liquid slowly evaporates, so for each year

that passes there is less and less whisky in the cask to be sold. This scarcity is compounded by the fact that production practices in Scottish distilleries have developed significantly since the turn of the 20th century, with particularly big changes occurring in the 1970s and late 1990s/early 2000s. Thus, as well as being rarer, the flavour of older whisky may significantly differ from whiskies made by the same distilleries today. The experience of drinking a spirit that would have been distilled in a memorable or celebratory year, such as the drinker's birth year, also adds to the charm of drinking Scotch.

All these factors do not necessarily mean that the whisky tastes better. Personal preference for flavour varies so much from person to person that it is difficult to say there is a whisky that everyone would love. Older whiskies are often 'smoother', more complex and more rounded by the cask's influence compared to younger whiskies, which often deliver more of a spritely, spirit-forward taste. However, an old whisky can also be overmatured, which can result in excess bitterness or the whisky being too tannic. If a drinker enjoys heavily peated whiskies, then younger spirits might be the better choice, as peaty characteristics tend to decline during maturation. What is more, the cask can sometimes overshadow the smoke as time goes on and give a character that is more balanced between smoke and the other spirit-derived and cask-derived flavours and aromas. There are plenty of peat fans around the world who think, when it comes to whisky, 'the smokier, the better', so they might prefer a young whisky that can carry a more powerful smoky taste than an older one would.

The flavour extraction also depends on the cask type. There are casks that particularly suit younger whiskies, as they can impart a relatively high amount of flavour during a shorter maturation. An STR cask (shaved, toasted and re-charred) is an example of a cask that is frequently used for whiskies from newer distilleries. Recently opened distilleries often start selling their whisky at a young age, when it might just be legal at three years old, to ensure they have a quicker turnaround of capital for the running and upkeep of the distillery to secure its future. Many distilleries release other products like gin, for example, while the whisky is maturing – but for a whisky distillery, it is, of course, the whisky that is the crown jewel.

It is the liquid-to-wood ratio that determines how much cask character the spirit will take on. A smaller cask, where the liquid proportionally has more access to the oak, will result in an enhanced extraction and more cask flavours in a shorter period of time compared to a larger cask. Should a distillery want to make an older whisky that still retains a lot of its spirit notes, for example with peated whisky, a less active cask or a larger cask with a lower spirit-to-oak ratio might be perfect.

Blended vs single malt vs single cask: which is better?

In the Scotch whisky world, there are a variety of terms that can describe a whisky, from blended whisky to single malt, depending on how it is made, how it is blended and where it comes from.

A single malt is whisky made from malted barley that has been mashed, fermented and distilled in copper pot stills at the same distillery. Distilleries are allowed to use any number of casks from that same distillery for the bottling, and it will always be classed as a single malt. Many single malts are therefore a blend of the contents of many different casks, but as long as they are all this type of whisky from the same distillery, the term 'single malt' is correct; a blended Scotch whisky is different. If a single malt is bottled using only spirit from a single cask, then it is both a single malt and a single cask whisky.

Then we have single grain whisky. Again, the 'single' in the name refers to the fact that the whisky comes from a single distillery. If it is a 100 per cent malted barley spirit from a pot still, then it is a single malt, but if you were to use any other grain, such as wheat, corn or rye, this would make it a grain whisky. For grain whisky, the spirit can be distilled in either pot stills or continuous stills, although the latter is more common. When a continuous still is used, the whisky is classed as single grain no matter if 100 per cent malted barley or a variety of different grains have been used, as long as the spirit all comes from one distillery.

The most popular category in Scotch whisky worldwide is blended Scotch whisky. A blended Scotch whisky consists of single malts and single grain whiskies that have been blended together. The single malts usually contribute flavour and body, while the grain whisky acts as a neutral base to lighten and highlight the malts. Blended Scotch whiskies tend to be made up of a higher proportion of grain whisky, but there are no rules for the quantities of each whisky type.

There are also blended malts and blended grains. A blended malt consists of a variety of single malts from different distilleries that have been blended, but it does not contain any grain whisky. A blended grain is the opposite and is instead

made of single grains from different distilleries that have been blended, and it has no single malt components. What distinguishes them from single malts or single grains is that these categories contain whisky from more than one distillery.

Though the term 'blended' is often seen as a sign of a less prestigious whisky, this is simply not true. Blends can be very versatile and are designed to have specific flavour profiles, from heavily peated to fruity and approachable, all depending on the whiskies that are used for it. Blended Scotch whiskies tend to be more affordable than single malts, as grain whisky is easier to produce in higher volumes. A big grain whisky distillery can produce in a couple of weeks what a medium-sized single malt distillery produces in a year.

The label on a whisky bottle will tell you the category of whisky and whether it is a single malt, as well as displaying the Scottish region that the distillery is located in. There are six main whisky-producing regions: the Highlands, the Islands (sometimes considered to be part of the Highlands), the Lowlands, Speyside, Campbeltown and Islay. Technically, Speyside is a region in the Highlands, so some Speyside whiskies can be labelled as Highland instead.

What do the age statements mean?

The age statement is the number on the bottle that tells you how old the youngest component in the whisky is. Common age statements include 10 years old, 12 years old and 18 years old, and they indicate the number of years the whisky has spent maturing in a cask. Whether it is a single malt, blended malt or grain whisky, the age statement is always indicative of the youngest whisky in that bottle. This means that a 12-year-old whisky can have older whisky blended into it, but as long as there is a proportion of 12-year-old, that is the number on the bottle. If someone purchases a 12-year-old whisky, it will remain a 12-year-old no matter how many years it sits in the bottle because the maturation stops as soon as the whisky leaves the cask. The oak contact is essential for Scotch whisky maturation, so a whisky bottle kept on a shelf will not increase its age statement or continue maturing.

There is still some prejudice towards younger whisky, and many people are under the impression that older is always better. However, it is not just about the age on the bottle, but rather the overall unique flavour of the whisky that really matters. Even though age statements above 10 years old might be more common, there are also younger age statements on the market. There are also whiskies in which the contents of the blend vary greatly between younger and much older whisky. Companies that bottle such blends often choose to release these expressions with a No Age Statement (NAS) and let the flavour speak for itself rather than indicate age. Alongside NAS and age statements there are also vintages. A vintage on a whisky label refers to the year the spirit was distilled and when the liquid was bottled. For example, if a whisky was distilled in 1995 and bottled in 2010, it is a 15-year-old whisky. Core releases are not often labelled with only vintages any more – they tend to be used for exclusive or special releases, and many whisky collectors find pleasure in trying or buying a bottle of whisky with the same vintage as a memorable year such as a birthday or celebration.

Finally, cask quality has improved, with more fresh casks like first-fill bourbon being used nowadays, in comparison with older casks used more frequently in the past. With fresher casks, the whisky can take on flavour and colour more quickly, so while an old refill cask might need 10 or 12 years to mature the whisky properly, a newer cask would need fewer.

Does whisky go off? And should you decant it?

When purchasing a bottle of whisky, there are plenty of interesting options on the shelves: various beautiful bottle designs and differing colours of glass and shape, each with its own unique charm. However, in the 19th century it was not the norm to purchase bottles of whisky from the merchants. Instead, customers would bring their own bottles to be filled directly from casks because glass was very expensive, so owning numerous glass bottles would have been a significant status symbol. To showcase who the bottles belonged to, they would often be decorated with the family crest. These bottles were not primarily meant for storage, but as a transportation vessel to get the whisky home, where it would then be poured into a decanter. As glass became more affordable, whisky began to be sold in individual bottles. As the century went on, and as glass continuously decreased in price and increased in quality, it became more and more common to serve whisky straight from a bottle rather than a decanter.

Many higher-end offerings are bottled in exclusive, extravagant constructions, especially those primarily meant to be decorative or a collector's piece. These bottles tend to be decadent display items, status symbols or bought as an investment to sell in later years.

Many people still love to display their whisky at home in a decanter. Pouring yourself, or serving a guest, a dram from a beautifully crafted decanter adds a little 'theatre' to the moment, as both the weight and look can heighten the experience. The charm of a decanter can be purely visual and there are many different designs to choose from, from crystal to hand-blown glass. Since some whiskies come bottled in coloured glass, decanting into a clear glass decanter can be a way to display the whisky's unique colour.

The optimal conditions for storing whisky are to keep it in darkness, standing up and ideally somewhere colder than room temperature. If a bottle has been opened, it should not be left for too long, as this can affect the flavour. An opened bottle can result in the whisky seeming more dull in its intensity and variety of flavours, as well as reducing the alcohol strength over time. The effects generally become more

impactful the higher the air-to-liquid ratio is. If a full-sized bottle only has a little bit left in it, it is often preferable to move it to a smaller bottle to limit the exposure to oxygen so that the spirit is more likely to keep its original character for longer.

When it comes to storage, a half-full decanter is not the best vessel for whisky that will be left on its own for a long period of time, as this will significantly expose the whisky to air in the decanter — not to mention that decanter lids often don't seal well. However, the same basic rules apply to decanters as to bottles. If the seal is good and the bottle is kept fairly full without too much oxygen contact and away from direct sunlight, then the whisky should not alter too much. However, even when kept in a closed and sealed bottle, the flavours and aromas of the spirit will change over time. Perhaps the best way to enjoy whisky is to drink it within a reasonable timescale.

Are all Scotch whiskies peated?

The simple answer is no. Most distilleries in Scotland focus purely on unpeated spirit, including Glenmorangie and The Macallan.

Peat is a naturally occurring organic material resembling soil, which is often found in wet conditions in places like bogs and moors. It is responsible for the smoky flavour that can be found in some Scotch whiskies. With only one or two exceptions, if peat is not used to smoke the grain used to make a whisky, then the whisky will not be smoky. When the barley is in the kiln, peat is added to the fire. The smoke released from the peat contains chemical compounds called phenols that attach to the barley when it is within a specific range of moisture content.

In Scotland you can also come across peated water, often quickly identified due to its brown colour; but, if peated water has any impact on whisky production at all, it is minimal and has no relation to smoky characteristics.

Some bottle labels state a range of ppm (phenol parts per million) levels, a measurement intended to help the drinker gauge the intensity of the peaty characteristics of the whisky. However, this figure almost always relates only to the grain and is not necessarily indicative of the final flavour, which is also influenced by the production process. Having said that, heavily peated whiskies are generally made from barley smoked to around 40–55 ppm and these tend to use 100 per cent peated malt. Some distilleries use only a small percentage of peated malt or barley smoked to a lesser degree, both of which result in a less smoky influence on aromas and flavours. Barley smoked to around 10ppm is considered lightly peated.

Some distilleries use peated malt just a couple of times a year, while others produce peated whisky exclusively all year round. For the former, it is usually in conjunction with their silent season, in which distilleries pause production to clean all equipment and undertake maintenance work. This is traditionally done in the summer months because distillery workers, who traditionally were also farmers, needed to attend to their farms and cut peat before they could start distillation up again after the harvest. The thorough cleaning in the silent season also ensures that there are no traces of peat left in the equipment, ready for the unpeated spirit runs to commence.

Certain regions are known for their peaty whiskies, such as Islay (see image opposite of Ardbeg distillery; see also page 167), a small island off Scotland's west coast, where a lot of peat bogs can be found. Many argue that peat from different parts of Scotland will create different aromas in the whisky because island peat contains more coastal vegetation, whereas mainland peat can consist of more heather, flowers and grass. This results in island peat tending to have a more coastal and medicinal character, whereas Highland peat can be more floral.

The misconception that all Scotch whiskies are peated might be based on the fact that peat was vital to many of the whisky distilleries of Scotland before the 20th century. It was the main heating source for homes as well as distilleries, as there were few trees growing in many rural areas of Scotland, and coal or gas were not widely available for fuel. Therefore, all distilleries that used peat to fire their kilns would produce whisky with some aromas of smoke. Nowadays other heating methods such as steam or hot water are used, which have no flavour impact on the whisky.

Can whisky be used in mixed drinks?

Whisky purists might believe that the only way to enjoy a Scotch whisky is neat, or possibly with the addition of a few drops of water or ice. However, whisky cocktails are extremely popular and several have assisted in the upswing in popularity of Scotch throughout the world.

The Golden Era of cocktails during the late 19th century saw the creation of many classic drinks. Around the end of the century, an American audience started appreciating smooth Scotch blended whiskies, thanks to blenders like Tommy Dewar and their innovative marketing ideas. Cocktails using Scotch, such as the Rob Roy, were invented. However, when Prohibition occurred in the 1920s in the USA, alcohol was harder to come by and to drink because it was not made in official distilleries any more, and needed other ingredients to mask the flavour rather than enhance it. A popular serve in the speakeasy bars was what was already termed the 'old fashioned' cocktail: a mix of ice, sugar, bitters and a brown spirit like whisky or rum, though by the 1920s many bartenders were adding muddled fruit. The Scotch and soda, or 'highball', also went underground. Since distilleries were forced to make alternative products or shut down during Prohibition, there was an increase in Scotch whisky sold illegally on the American black market during this period. The only way people could drink whisky legally was if it was prescribed by a doctor for medicinal purposes.

When Prohibition ended, cocktails soared to mainstream popularity again, partly as a result of well-known names like Ernest Hemingway, who wrote not only about daiquiris and negronis, but also the 'Scotch & Soda'. The whisky highball was a popular drink of choice for a long time, but eventually other serves like Vodka Soda became trendy and took over on the scene. The whisky highball was extremely popular in Japan after being introduced as a casual drink for after work, and it remains a favoured drink today, often served alongside food. In fact, highballs are making a comeback among whisky drinkers all over the world and can be a refreshing alternative to a neat dram or a pleasant drink for those who do not enjoy drinking strong spirits on their own. Other classic highball cocktails include Whisky Ginger, which uses ginger ale as a mixer, or the well-known Whiskey Coke ('whiskey' with an 'e' usually refers to American or Irish), in which cola is the second component.

Nowadays more elevated highball recipes are becoming common, featuring a longer list of ingredients. Often, highballs can be designed to accentuate or contrast specific flavours of the whisky or spirit that is being used. The highball is a perfect contender for experimentation with flavour, as the character can be changed depending on what whisky is used, what mixer and if other ingredients such as flavoured syrups or liqueurs are added. The Prisma on page 46 is a particularly well-crafted example of a whisky highball.

How to Mix and Serve Whisky

Scotch whisky can be served in a variety of ways. When ordering Scotch in a bar, it is usually presented in a Glencairn glass or a whisky tumbler alongside a small jug of water and the option of ice ('on the rocks') or no ice. These glasses facilitate appreciation of the spirit as well as an enjoyable drinking experience. A tumbler can also be used to serve spirit-forward cocktails, also known as short cocktails. Examples of spirit-forward cocktails include the Old Fashioned, Rob Roy, The Godfather and Rusty Nail. With the exception of the Old Fashioned (made generally with bourbon), the other three cocktails mentioned are usually prepared with Scotch whisky. A Rob Roy is the Scotch whisky version of a Manhattan, which was originally made with American rye whiskey. Only two ingredients – Scotch whisky and almond liqueur – are needed to make The Godfather, a popular cocktail throughout the 1970s and probably named after the famous crime film that dominated screens across the USA following its release in 1972. The Rusty Nail consists primarily of Scotch whisky and the Scotch whisky liqueur Drambuie; the recipe can be adjusted by changing the ratio between the two.

Another classic glass for whisky serves is the straight-sided, narrow highball glass, which is similar in shape to a collins glass, although smaller. Both of these glasses are used to serve so-called 'long' drinks, like the Scotch & Soda or Whisky & Ginger, which contain a higher quantity of a mixer (often a 2:1 or 3:1 ratio of mixer to spirit) than those presented in a tumbler or old fashioned glass. Usually, a highball glass is called for when only spirit, mixer and ice are required. Meanwhile, the capacity of the larger collins glass allows for additional ingredients such as fruit or citrus juice – just as is required for its namesake cocktail, the Tom Collins.

A vast number of Scotch whisky cocktails have been invented throughout history, and the glassware used for them can be as creative as the serves themselves. A couple of classics worth mentioning are hot serves such as the

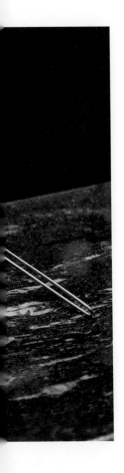

Hot Toddy, Scotch Coffee and Blue Blazer. A footed coffee glass with a handle tends to be used for these, since they are served hot. The classic Hot Toddy contains whisky, honey, lemon and tea or alternatively hot water. Traditionally it was believed that hot toddies had medicinal properties, which perhaps harks back to the days when all three ingredients were considered to be good for treating illness. It is also popular to use various spices in hot toddies, such as ginger, cloves, cinnamon or nutmeg, or even teas (chai is a popular choice). The Hot Toddy can be varied in flavour by choosing different whiskies or tea varieties, or by switching the more common blossom honey for an aromatic heather honey. The Scotch Coffee is the Scottish version of its cousin from Ireland, the main difference being that Scotch whisky is used instead of Irish whiskey. Finally, the Blue Blazer is a mixture of sugar, boiling water and Scotch, the latter of which is ignited before being mixed into the drink by passing it between silver-plated mugs.

As we have seen, Scotch whisky is tremendously versatile and it will not be a surprise that serves are becoming increasingly creative and experimental, as bartenders and enthusiasts explore which flavours pair well with whisky; modern mixer ideas include birch water and coconut water. In comparison to adding just water to a dram, birch water and coconut water can impart new flavour to the whisky, which normal tap or spring water, in theory, should not. Birch water is sap tapped straight from birch trees and tends to have a crisp character with natural, fresh sweetness. Coconut water, on the other hand, which is the clear liquid from inside a young coconut, has a salty, nutty and sweet character, but can also be described as sour if the fruit is very young.

Whisky can truly be served in any way the drinker prefers, which makes it a very versatile drink, suitable for many different palates, including in the exclusive SCOTCH cocktail recipes that follow. Each recipe features the particular whisky that our Whisky Ambassadors like to use, but feel free to use whichever bottle you have to hand.

Prisma

The Prisma is an incredibly refreshing cocktail and relatively easy to prepare once the cordial is made. Whisky cocktails can be perceived as relatively strong and unapproachable, but this highball is quite the opposite. Pairing a light, fresh Speyside whisky with peach and aniseed (anise) will elevate the sweetness of the drink. The acidity ensures that the drink is balanced and is a perfect replacement for a crisp glass of white wine during the warm summer months. This fabulously efficient serve is also great for gatherings, as it is a preparation-heavy drink. It allows quick service and means you can spend more time entertaining guests as a result.

35ml (1¼fl oz) The Macallan 12 year old Double Cask

20ml (³/₅fl oz) Tarragon Green Tea Cordial (see adjacent or use 20ml/³/₅fl oz) lemon ice tea and 4 drops anise spirit)

2 drops Ms Better's Mt. Fuji Bitters (or any other fruity bitters)

150ml (5fl oz) peach soda (we use DASH peach sparkling water)

purple shiso sprig, to garnish (optional)

Put the whisky in a highball glass with the Tarragon Green Tea Cordial and bitters. Fill the glass with ice cubes, then top up with the peach soda. Finally, garnish with a sprig of purple shiso, if you like.

Tarragon Green Tea Cordial

Brew 500ml (18fl oz) green tea, ideally using water boiled to about 80°C (176°F), infused to about double the strength you would drink it at. Once the teabags or leaves have been removed, add 50g (1¾ oz) fresh tarragon, muddle lightly and leave to cool. Once cooled, strain to remove the tarragon and add 5g (¹/₈ oz) malic acid (lemon juice can be used as an alternative). Shake well to dissolve the acid, then add 250ml (9fl oz) agave nectar. Store in a sterilised bottle – it should last for around 1 month in the fridge.

Belgravia

This is a fantastic cocktail for using what is often considered a waste product to make something incredibly simple and tasty. Suitable for summer, due to the refreshing zingy notes, or winter, thanks to the richer flavours provided by the cherry cordial. This is a fantastic take on a classic Whisky Sour!

50ml (1¾fl oz) Glenfiddich 15 year old

30ml (1fl oz) cherry cordial (see adjacent or use a shop-bought alternative)

25ml (⁴/₅fl oz) egg white or aquafaba

bottled cherries and a crumbled dried lavender sprig, to garnish

Put all the ingredients in a cocktail shaker and shake to mix everything together. Add a handful of ice cubes and shake until the cocktail is well chilled and diluted. Double strain into a rocks glass or short tumbler filled with ice cubes. Garnish with cherries and lavender.

Cherry Cordial

This cordial is made with cherry syrup from good-quality canned or bottled cherries. First, strain the cherries and collect the syrup. Weigh the syrup and add 4 per cent of its weight of malic acid (lemon juice can be used as an alternative). Store in a sterilised bottle – it should last for around 3 weeks in the fridge.

Far Side
of the World

CAMERON SAYS

This variation on a classic Boulevardier plays on the sweeter notes usually found in American whiskies, but allows exploration of flavour combinations highlighted by Scotch whisky. The bitter element in Campari works extremely well in balancing out the sweet and oily texture created by the coconut infusion, which needs to be made in advance.

20g (¾ oz) desiccated coconut (or unsweetened shredded coconut)

45ml (1½fl oz) Glencadam 15 year old

35ml (1¼fl oz) Italian vermouth

20ml (³/₅fl oz) Campari

strip of lime zest, to garnish

To prepare the whisky, preheat the oven to 180°C fan (400°F), Gas Mark 6. Spread the desiccated coconut onto a baking tray and bake until the coconut just colours. Be careful not to burn the coconut, or this will make the cocktail bitter. Once cooled, transfer to a container, add the whisky and allow to infuse for an hour. Strain through a coffee filter twice and chill in the fridge.

To make the cocktail, pour all ingredients into a mixing glass with large ice cubes and stir until the liquid is ice cold. Strain into a rocks glass or short tumbler filled with ice cubes. Twist the lime zest over the glass so that the essential oils spray into the liquid, and drop it into the drink.

The Clear Conscience

This is the perfect cold cocktail to warm you up on a winter evening. The spicy notes make it refreshing yet warming. The ginger spice works incredibly well with the subtle smoke found in the spritz and the Johnnie Walker Black Label.

50ml (1¾fl oz) Johnnie Walker Black Label

20ml (³/₅fl oz) ginger liqueur (The King's Ginger is a good option)

30ml (1fl oz) Honey Cordial (see adjacent)

2 dashes orange bitters

75ml (2½fl oz) spicy ginger beer

long, thin slice of red chilli and strip of orange zest, to garnish

spritz of Talisker 10 year old (optional)

Combine the whisky, ginger liqueur and Honey Cordial in a cocktail shaker, add ice cubes and shake vigorously to chill. Once cold, strain into a stemmed beer glass filled with large ice cubes. Add the orange bitters and top up with the ginger beer. Garnish with red chilli and orange zest. Spray a touch of the Talisker over the top of the glass.

Honey Cordial

Mix 2 parts honey with 1 part boiling water until the honey is dissolved. Add 1 star anise and some orange zest and let it infuse to your taste. Store in a clean, sterilised bottle – it should last for around 3 weeks in the fridge.

Parcel of Rogues

An exceptional whisky, such as The Balvenie 21 year old PortWood, can be used in a cocktail that complements the complex flavours of the single malt without overpowering them. The flavours of the additions are light enough to accentuate the fresh berry influence the ex-port casks have on this well-aged whisky. It is the perfect example of why single malts should occasionally be considered as ingredients as well as finished products.

35ml (1¼fl oz) The Balvenie 21 year old PortWood

20ml (³/₅fl oz) Cocchi Americano Rosa or other rosé vermouth

2 dashes pineapple and star anise bitters

5ml (¹/₆fl oz) jasmine syrup (we use William Fox)

star anise, to garnish

Put all the ingredients in a chilled mixing glass. Add large ice cubes and stir until chilled. Once chilled, strain into a frozen Nick and Nora glass (a small stemmed cocktail glass) and garnish with a whole star anise.

Concerto

This Rob Roy variation plays on the toasty and nutty notes of the Tamdhu single malt to create a very intriguing and luxurious cocktail. The use of sesame paste adds incredible texture to the cocktail and the unusual addition of pickled walnut delivers enough acidity to cut through the richness.

50ml (1¾fl oz) black sesame-washed Tamdhu 15 year old (see below)

25ml (⁴/₅fl oz) Italian vermouth

2 dashes chocolate or cocoa bitters

2 dashes black walnut bitters (optional)

slice of pickled walnut, to garnish

To prepare the whisky, add 5g (1 teaspoon) black sesame paste and 50ml (1¾fl oz) Tamdhu 15 year old to a cocktail shaker, shake to ensure the paste is incorporated into the whisky and leave to stand for 2 hours. Pour into a sealed freezerproof container, leaving some room at the top, and freeze for 2 hours. Once chilled, strain through a coffee filter to remove the paste.

To make the cocktail, pour all the ingredients into a mixing glass and add large ice cubes. Stir to chill and dilute. Once ice cold, strain into a cocktail glass and garnish with a slice of pickled walnut.

Pomona Horizon

This cocktail pays tribute to the 'Auld Alliance' between Scotland and France. It is the ideal cocktail to serve during autumn gatherings, as both plums and apples are perfectly in season. This can be batched ahead of time and topped up with cider and Champagne for a quick and easy crowd-pleasing serve.

25ml (⁴/₅fl oz) yellow plum-infused Glen Moray 18 year old (see below)

15ml (¹/₂fl oz) cider brandy

10ml (¹/₃fl oz) white verjus (or, use 5ml/¹/₆fl oz apple cider vinegar and 5ml/¹/₆fl oz apple juice)

1 teaspoon apricot jam

50ml (1 ¾fl oz) dry cider

50ml (1 ¾fl oz) Champagne

canned or bottled mini apple or apple slice, to garnish

To prepare the whisky, add 3.5g (½ teaspoon) dried yellow plums and 25ml (⁴/₅fl oz) Glen Moray 18 year old to a sealed container and allow to infuse for 2–3 hours at room temperature. Strain through a coffee filter to remove the plums and chill the infusion in the fridge.

To make the cocktail, place the first 4 ingredients in a cocktail shaker filled with ice cubes and shake well to chill. Once chilled, double strain into a small wine glass and top up with the cider and Champagne. Garnish with a mini apple or apple slice.

Chronicle

CAMERON SAYS

The recognisable passion fruit and vanilla flavour combination in this cocktail is a great use of the sweet, fruity nature of single grain whisky and elevates it into a drink that really is a crowd pleaser. This is great for summer and can be served in a Champagne glass or wine glass as an aperitivo.

25ml (⁴/₅fl oz) passion fruit and vanilla-infused Compass Box Hedonism whisky (see below)

10ml (¹/₃fl oz) rosé vermouth

2 drops Peychaud's bitters

75ml (2 ¹/₂fl oz) rosé Champagne

50ml (1 ¾fl oz) soda water

half a passion fruit and a few sage leaves, to garnish

To make the infusion, scrape out a quarter of the pulp from a passion fruit and add it to a cocktail shaker with 25ml (⁴/₅fl oz) of Compass Box Hedonism whisky. Shake and let it stand for 15 minutes, then pour into a freezerproof container and freeze for 2 hours. Once infused, add a pinch of seeds from 1 vanilla pod (bean) and strain through a coffee filter.

To make the cocktail, put the homemade infusion, rosé vermouth and Peychaud's bitters in a glass. Fill with large ice cubes and mix gently to ensure it is all combined. Top up with the rosé Champagne and soda water and garnish with half a passion fruit and a few sage leaves.

OUR TOP 100 WHISKIES

The following is by no means an exhaustive summary of SCOTCH's collection, or of the staggering range of Scotch whisky now available to purchase both in Scotland and abroad. Head Whisky Ambassador Cameron Ewen has, however, chosen 100 of the most exciting bottles behind the SCOTCH bar that you can sample, should you choose to visit, or alternatively secure for your own collection, suitable for all palates and price points. Each bottle features an insight into the distillery or independent bottler that produces or sells it, as well as Cameron's own tasting notes and comments.

Scotland is traditionally divided into five or six whisky regions: **Highlands** (see pages 65–105), **Speyside** (see pages 106–154), **Islands** (see pages 155–166), **Islay** (see pages 167–183), **Lowlands** (see pages 184–189) and **Campeltown** (see pages 190–200). The whiskies have been organised according to the map and key on pages 6–7, with an extra section included for **Blends/Grains/ Independent Bottlers** (see pages 201–214).

Aberfeldy

Aberfeldy distillery can be found where Perthshire's tallest mountain, deepest loch and longest glen meet. This Highland distillery was built in 1898 by John Alexander Dewar on a site that originally housed a brewery. It is located only a couple of miles away from where his father, John Dewar, was born and is the only Scotch whisky distillery built by the Dewar family. The Dewar name was already well known for Dewar's blended whiskies, but the company was dependent on buying whisky to supply their bottlings. Owning a distillery meant a reliable source for single malts, which could also be sold and traded with others if needed. The Victorian building was designed by the famous distillery architect Charles Chree Doig, and its former maltings features his iconic pagoda-shaped ventilator on its rooftop. The Pitilie Burn, which runs into the River Tay, is used as the water source, and both the wash stills and spirit stills are onion shaped. The land surrounding the distillery was once known for its deposits of gold, leading to the Aberfeldy single malt being referred to as the Golden Dram. Aberfeldy whisky is bottled as a single malt and used as a component in Dewar's blended whiskies, which is one of the bestselling blended Scotch brands in America.

ABERFELDY
18 year old

Single malt

PRICE ●●●●○

ABV 43%

NOSE Having been finished in Tuscan red wine casks, the whisky immediately offers sour cherry and bitter almonds before revealing a sweet candied orange note.

TASTE Continues with the fruit characteristics on the nose and adds layers of subtle oak and fresh lively lime.

FINISH The finish is direct and spicy, and leaves an elegant oak influence.

Comments

Trying Aberfeldy's red wine cask collection is a rewarding deviation from the classic American oak maturation the distillery is famous for. It is great to see the effect of different wine casks on the subtle spirit produced at Aberfeldy.

ABERFELDY
21 year old

Single malt

PRICE ●●●●○

ABV 40%

NOSE The influence of high-quality bourbon casks is evident here, with amazing notes of fresh lemon, orange zest and white peach.

TASTE Vanilla becomes a lot more apparent on the palate along with delicate and fragrant oak influence, providing a thick and luxurious texture.

FINISH The fruit is joined by a soft smoke, slight dried fruit, rich whisky-laden sultanas and the ever-present citrus.

Comments

This was one of the first whiskies I tried in which the texture and richness of the whisky was most noticeable. The thickness really does help carry the delicate flavours of this beautiful Highland whisky.

Ardnamurchan

The Ardnamurchan (pronounced 'Ard-na-*mur*-cun') distillery was officially opened by HRH The Princess Royal in July 2014. The distillery is owned by independent bottler Adelphi and gets its name from the Ardnamurchan peninsula where it is located, the most westerly point of mainland Scotland. Since its beginning, the distillery has had a clear focus on its green credentials, resulting in Ardnamurchan being considered one of the most sustainable distilleries in Scotland. The heating and electricity used by the distillery come from local sources through a biomass boiler and a hydrogenerator located in a nearby river. Every bottle of Ardnamurchan whisky allows customers to track the various steps of its manufacture online via a QR code printed on the bottle. This is just one example of how Ardnamurchan is leading the way as an innovative distillery.

ARDNAMURCHAN
Paul Launois
2023 Release

Single malt

PRICE ●●○○○

ABV 57.1%

NOSE The oak influence is incredibly subtle, allowing the wine cask to really express itself. Sweet white grapes and preserved orange are apparent.

TASTE Delicate dry vanilla, cinnamon and nutmeg are all present, with dried apricots providing more fruit character.

FINISH There is spice coming from the oak in the form of fragrant cooking spices. The spirit character adds cracked black pepper, leading to a long, lingering and very intriguing finish.

Comments

Fans or regular drinkers of Ardnamurchan will be used to the distillery's mildly peated releases that showcase the rugged west coast location the distillery calls home. This release is unpeated to allow the beautiful influence of 195-litre (51.5-US-gallon) barriques from Domaine Paul Launois to complement the fruit-driven distillate.

Balblair

Balblair is one of the oldest distilleries in the northern Highlands, and was first founded in 1790 by the Ross family near Edderton. In 1872, the distillery was rebuilt and moved to its present site nearby, an ancient Pictish gathering place overlooking the Dornoch Firth, in order to be closer to the new railway. The distillery sits right next to the Clach Biorach standing stone, believed to have been a landmark for over 4,000 years. The stone is engraved with an iconic Pictish Z-rod symbol, which also decorates the Balblair bottles to honour the historic land around the distillery.

The distillery was mothballed in 1911, and was commandeered by the army during the second World War, but production eventually resumed in 1949. Balblair runs a long and slow production, with a 62-hour fermentation and a 4½-hour distillation to create its light yet complex spirit. Inver House Distillers purchased Balblair in 1996, and in 2019 the distillery rebranded its core releases from vintages to age statements alongside a new bottle design.

BALBLAIR
18 year old

Single malt

PRICE ●●●●○

ABV 46%

NOSE There is completeness in this whisky. A beautiful roundness with no major spikes in flavour. Light caramel, orchard fruits and ginger are all in evidence.

TASTE Juicy stone fruits and spice provided by two types of oak reveal themselves with cinnamon sugar-dusted apples and vanilla crème.

FINISH Short but rewarding, with classic baking spices coming from the sherry cask influence.

Comments

Since the Balblair range moved away from vintage whiskies and introduced age statements, this 18-year-old has been consistently excellent. The balance of American and European oak influence is superb, and this is a whisky that suits a number of different occasions.

Clynelish

The original Clynelish (pronounced 'cline-lish') distillery was founded in 1819 by the Marquess of Stafford, later the Duke of Sutherland. The distillery sits a few miles away from the village of Brora and the northeast coastline of Scotland. This location has been the site of continuous whisky production through wars and economic depressions, albeit in two different distillery buildings.

A second distillery, known as Clynelish 2 or Clynelish B, was built next door to the original site in the 1960s, and the older distillery was later briefly mothballed before reopening as Brora distillery. Brora was finally closed in 1983 before being refurbished and reopened in 2021. It is Clynelish B, now simply known as Clynelish, that produces the Clynelish spirit we know today.

The whisky from Clynelish is unpeated and recognised for its unique waxy character, which is credited to the natural build-up of residual oils in the feints receiver and prized for its use in blends.

In 2021, the distillery opened its doors to a new visitor experience, part of the £150 million investment by Diageo to reshape its Scotch whisky visitor experiences across multiple distilleries, and the new Johnnie Walker Princes Street whisky experience in Edinburgh. The distillery is the Highland home of Johnnie Walker and part of Diageo's Four Corners of Scotland distillery collection that contributes to the Johnnie Walker range of blended Scotch whiskies.

CLYNELISH
12 year old
Special Release 2022

Single malt

PRICE ●●●●○

ABV 58.5%

NOSE This is a great example of a rich northern Highland distillery expression, showcasing dried pineapple and orange peel before sweeter caramels and vanilla come forward.

TASTE A beautiful texture coats the mouth with fresh cream and soft, whisky-soaked apricots. Spice then appears with a touch of habanero chilli and fragrant ginger.

FINISH The finish is extremely long in this example of Clynelish. The classic waxiness of the distillery is ever present and allows the taste of the whisky to change over time.

Comments

Clynelish is one of those distilleries where you look for certain attributes in its whisky. This expression is a great example of that style: rich, full-bodied and waxy, yet still retaining some fruitiness. The addition of a finishing period in Pedro Ximénez sherry casks has amplified the rich and fruity qualities of the distillery with great results.

Dalwhinnie

The Dalwhinnie distillery, originally called Strathspey, was built in 1897 right next to the railway that connected the central belt to Speyside and the Highlands. The name Dalwhinnie is thought to be derived from *dail chuinnidh* in Scottish Gaelic, which roughly means 'meeting place' – a fitting name considering that Dalwhinnie sits near the junction of multiple sizable drove roads where ancient cattle drovers would meet on their way through the mountains. Nowadays, the arterial A9 passes by and the distillery can be spotted from the road with its iconic pagoda-style rooftops. Dalwhinnie is one of the highest distilleries in Scotland and runs its production in some of the coldest conditions in the country, with a yearly average temperature of around 6°C (43°F). The distillery is considered fairly remote, in spite of its Highland location between the Lowlands and Speyside and the fact that it is well connected by both rail and road. The distillery sources its water, a combination of melted snow and rainwater, from Lochan na Doire-uaine in the Drumochter Hills. The whisky from Dalwhinnie distillery gets its sulphury and slightly waxy character from using clear instead of cloudy wort and long fermentation in combination with rapid condensation in wooden worm-tub condensers (see page 119) that limit copper contact. The worm tubs run naturally cold due to the low ambient temperature.

DALWHINNIE
30 year old
Special Release 2019

Single malt

PRICE ●●●●●

ABV 54.7%

NOSE Classic Dalwhinnie honey and spice, but enhanced after three decades of ageing. There is a note of morning cereal and sweetened cream also in evidence.

TASTE The directness of this whisky in the sweetened cream note is most noticeable, with a touch of damp cut grass minerality.

FINISH The length of ageing and alcohol strength in this whisky is presented elegantly and provides beautiful spice with white pepper and green chilli.

Comments

Dalwhinnie 30 year old is a perfect example of Diageo's Special Releases, an annual range of limited bottles from selected distilleries owned by the company. It provides a snapshot of what this beautiful Highland distillery was producing at a specific moment in time. After 30 years of careful maturation, this has become a fantastic whisky that showcases Dalwhinnie's distillery character.

Deanston

Deanston is located outside of Doune in what was once a cotton mill that employed around 1,500 people from the local area. The mill had to shut down in 1965, but Deanston founder Brodie Hepburn purchased the building with the idea of turning it into a distillery. The River Teith, which runs right by the distillery, is not just the water source, but also powers hydroelectric turbines in the building. These generate enough power to run the distillery, offices, the visitor centre and café, and contribute to making the distillery more sustainable. Unlike most distilleries, Deanston is unusual in having an open-top mash tun, a traditional feature in which the mash tun does not have a 'lid'. Deanston was also one of the first distilleries to bottle organic whisky, for which every step of the process, from barley to production and maturation, must be certified as organic.

DEANSTON
15 year old
Tequila Cask Finish

Single malt

PRICE ●●●○○

ABV 52.5%

NOSE A fruit salad of fresh tropical fruits begins, complemented by coconut and light oak spice derived from the cask.

TASTE Initially the influence of the tequila cask is noticeable with green leafy vegetables and sweet agave. A slight nuttiness also presents itself with sweet almonds or marzipan.

FINISH This whisky ends spicy and long. Nutmeg, cinnamon and ginger are all very evident.

Comments

This is the first time Deanston has used a tequila cask to age whisky, bringing the Highlands of Scotland and the Highlands of Jalisco, Mexico, together in one bottle. The finished product is a fantastic blend of both heritages – the agave is conspicuous and really intriguing.

DEANSTON
18 year old

Single malt

PRICE ●●●○○

ABV 46.3%

NOSE After 18 years of ageing in American oak, there is an abundance of citrus fruit, barley sugar and cereal sweetness.

TASTE Beeswax and lemon curd are most apparent, creating a light yet full-bodied whisky. At the end of the palate there is a touch of spice in the form of soft candied ginger.

FINISH Long, elegant and sweet. Lots of freshness here, which highlights the waxy, honeyed character that Deanston is famed for.

Comments

This whisky is, in my opinion, a wonderful example of how unobtrusive ageing can highlight the best of distillery character. One type of cask has been used and the whisky has been bottled at the perfect age to show balance between cask influence and waxy distillery character.

DEANSTON
21 year old
Fino Sherry Cask Finish

Single malt

PRICE ●●●●○

ABV 50.9%

NOSE This is a richer style of Deanston. Rum-soaked raisins, malt loaf and cinnamon are all apparent.

TASTE The palate is rich, full-bodied and fragrant. There is espresso coffee with delicate honeysuckle, pistachio and Amarena cherries.

FINISH The sweetness tails off and the finish is drying, leaving oak spice and bitter dark chocolate.

Comments

The clever use of casks shifts the distillery character in a less-explored direction for Deanston. After 21 years in bourbon casks, the rich yet dry influence of top-quality fino sherry casks was a welcome surprise when I tasted this excellent, spice-led limited edition.

Fettercairn

A Scottish landowner by the name of Sir Alexander Ramsay acquired a licence for Fettercairn distillery in 1824 after being a part of the movement campaigning for the introduction of Scotch whisky distillation licences in the 19th century. This canny businessman realised that he could hire illicit distillers who already had the skills and knowledge he needed to get his distillery off to a good start. In fact, Fettercairn has done things differently throughout its existence. In the mid 1950s, after a series of trials, the distillery team realised that running water along the outside of the stills would cool down the copper and increase condensation. This had the effect of increasing 'reflux' in the still and only allowing the lighter vapours to make it up the neck and over into the lyne arm to be collected. This practical solution to producing a lighter spirit was put in place by fashioning a copper tube around the upper part of the still that continuously cools the still with running water. These so-called 'water jackets' remain in place on the stills today and contribute to the tropical new make spirit of Fettercairn. The distillery rebranded in 2018 and the new bottle design incorporates a teal colour to reference the shade of oxidised copper that is common in distilleries. The brand is still decorated by the classic Ramsay clan crest, and several design details subtly bring attention to Fettercairn's whisky-making process.

FETTERCAIRN
18 year old
Scottish Oak

Single malt

PRICE ●●●●○

ABV 46.8%

NOSE Sweet and tropical with passion fruit and mango backed up with some amazing resinous oak. Nutmeg, cinnamon and cardamom add spice.

TASTE The fruitiness continues but dries out with dried mango and a touch of mocha. Dark cherry and raspberries add even more fruitiness.

FINISH The finish is long on the palate and the dark bitter chocolate really increases, yet there is also an incredible creaminess – almost like a liquid *pain suisse*.

Comments

Fettercairn's unique distillation process, in which water is run down the outside of the still to create a light and fruity spirit, has been nurtured and bolstered here by the clever use of Scottish oak as a finishing cask. The distillery is a pioneer in the use of Scottish oak and is on a mission to make it much more prevalent in Scotch whisky making.

FETTERCAIRN
22 year old

Single malt

PRICE ●●●●○

ABV 47%

NOSE An unmistakable aroma of green banana and tart green apples is noticeable at first. Fragrant oak and cut grass are also present.

TASTE The distillery's fruit-forward style is particularly apparent in this release, with juicy pineapple and more green apple.

FINISH The finish is long and lingering, the fruit increases and this is perhaps one of the juiciest and most exotic whiskies ever bottled.

Comments

Fettercairn has carved a new path based on the distillery's dedication to producing fruit-led whiskies of exceptional quality. The commitment to cask selection is clear after the rebrand, and there are some truly marvellous whiskies coming out of this Highland distillery. The 22-year-old is one of them.

Glencadam

Glencadam distillery opened in 1825 and almost seems to have frozen in time, as so little has changed in the almost two centuries since it started. This Highland distillery is located in Brechin, a town near the east coast, and is the last remaining traditional whisky distillery in Angus. Its neighbour Arbikie, near Montrose, is part of the 'new wave' of craft distillers. Glencadam was mothballed in 2000, but reopened in 2003 when the family-owned spirits company Angus Dundee Distillers acquired it.

In 2021, a working water wheel was reinstalled at the distillery, which is a nod to how it was powered back in its early days. To create its tropical and orchard fruit-forward spirit, Glencadam favours a production style that encourages reflux, which concentrates the lighter vapours in the new make spirit. This is achieved in part thanks to the lyne arms, which are on a 15-degree angle upwards, making it harder for heavier vapours to travel all the way up and over inside the stills.

GLENCADAM
15 year old

Single malt

PRICE ●●○○○

ABV 46%

NOSE Immediately there is orchard fruit with fresh, sweet red apples and lightly spiced custard. There is also an aniseed (anise)-like spice present in the nose. This is a really intriguing dram.

TASTE The fresh fruit continues on the palate with soft apricot and spiced apple. The creaminess starts to show itself.

FINISH Long and lingering finish with the apple transforming into pear alongside clove syrup.

Comments

For me, Glencadam is an incredible quality and a very versatile spirit that works in American or European oak casks. This should be a staple on any Scotch whisky enthusiast's shelf.

GLENCADAM
18 year old

Single malt

PRICE ●●●●○

ABV 46%

NOSE Rich and distinguished notes of stone fruit, pear and apple as well as creamy notes to complement the fruit. There is eggnog spiced with nutmeg and freshly cut orange.

TASTE The creaminess is prevalent on the palate with caramelised lemon and charred peach.

FINISH Gingerbread and pears in honey provide a tremendous end to this whisky, showcasing more of the orchard fruit character of the distillery.

Comments

It is great to see the reintroduction of Glencadam 18 year old after a small absence. The orchard fruit character of the distillery really does develop beautifully with increased age. This example highlights the distillery's strength when aged in American oak.

The GlenDronach

As a pioneer of sherry cask maturation, The GlenDronach is known for its sherried style of whisky, which has led to the distillery gaining quite a cult following. It was founded in 1826 and was one of the first distilleries in Scotland to obtain a licence after the passing of the Excise Act in 1823. Although it is located very close to the Speyside region, it is classed as a Highland distillery. The GlenDronach is in many ways considered a traditional distillery with its wooden washbacks and classic Porteus mill; it converted to steam heating the stills only in 2005, having used coal fire up until then. The distillery was mothballed in 1996, but reopened in 2002. Since then it has been under the ownership of both Chivas Brothers and the Benriach Distillery Company, which was later acquired by Brown Forman in 2016, adding The GlenDronach to its extensive spirits portfolio alongside Benriach and Glenglassaugh.

Today the whiskies are looked after by the dedicated distillery team along with the skilled palate of master blender Rachel Barrie, who has more than 30 years' experience of blending Scotch whisky.

THE GLENDRONACH
15 year old

Single malt

PRICE ●●●○○

ABV 46%

NOSE A burst of cherry, blackberry and oak. There is a pronounced nutty quality that delivers oily walnuts and bitter almonds.

TASTE The cherry continues with the addition of demerara sugar and dark chocolate to complement it. The sherry casks used in this expression have influenced this whisky particularly strongly.

FINISH The GlenDronach offers a long and spiced finish, with some bitter orange and oily walnut qualities emerging.

Comments

The GlenDronach has a fantastic reputation among fans of rich, Highland-style whiskies and I feel it is rightfully deserved. Their dedication to sourcing excellent and active sherry casks, be it oloroso or Pedro Ximénez, honours the style of whisky that has made the distillery so famous.

THE GLENDRONACH
21 year old

Single malt

PRICE ●●●●○

ABV 48%

NOSE Antique leather and blackcurrants immediately fill the glass. Rum-soaked dates and walnuts also introduce themselves.

TASTE The use of Pedro Ximénez casks for this whisky gives a terrifically rich sweetness. Turkish coffee served with a slice of nougat.

FINISH The strength of this whisky lends itself well to cutting through the richness and introduces a touch of cracked pepper.

Comments

The 21-year-old 'Parliament', named as such after the colony or parliament of rooks that have called the distillery grounds home for over 200 years, is a fantastic expression from The GlenDronach. Utilising both oloroso and Pedro Ximénez sherry casks, this is sweet, refined and mature.

THE GLENDRONACH
Grandeur 28 year old

Single malt

PRICE ●●●●●

ABV 48.9%

NOSE Ginger-spiced plum and chocolate-covered liquorice before freshly brewed espresso presents itself.

TASTE The texture of this whisky is impressive, mouth-coating and full-bodied. There is waxed leather and dark cherries, with the espresso becoming even more apparent.

FINISH The finish is long, lingering and bold. More of the spices reveal themselves at this point, along with candied ginger and extremely dark chocolate.

Comments

Since the release of The GlenDronach Grandeur series, dedicated to showcasing well-aged expressions from the distillery, very few have been short of outstanding. This expression is no different. Expertly nurtured in fino sherry casks and presented at cask strength, this is an older, rarely seen style of whisky.

Glen Garioch

Located at Oldmeldrum in Aberdeenshire, whisky has been made at the site of
Glen Garioch distillery since 1797. The distillery's name, which derives from the
name of the surrounding area and means 'place of roughness', is a regular source
of confusion. It is correctly pronounced 'glen-*gear*-ee' in the local dialect Doric.

Glen Garioch has changed ownership several times during its more than 200 years
of existence and, like many others, had to suspend production during the Second
World War. Post-war grain rationing limited production for many distilleries, and
it was not until the start of the 1960s that Glen Garioch was back to its pre-war
production level. To address issues with chronic water shortage, in 1972 the
distillery team employed a water diviner to find a new water source. A spring was
found on a neighbouring farm that could neither be seen nor heard. Dubbed the
Silent Spring, it was an abundant source that would assist in increasing production.
This led to expansion, as another still was added, followed by a fourth the following
year. In 1973 Glen Garioch was released as a single malt for the first time. Until
1995, when the distillery was closed for renovations, it produced a lightly peated
spirit using a proportion of malt from its own floor maltings, but switched to using
only externally supplied unpeated malt in the years to follow. Before this time, the
distillery's stills had been directly fired by gas burners. After renovations in late
2020, direct firing (similar to heating a pan over the flame of a cooker) has been
reinstated instead of using a copper coil to heat the still from the inside. Another
change has been a reduction in the number of stills from four to three.

GLEN GARIOCH
12 year old

Single malt

PRICE ●○○○○

ABV 48%

NOSE Freshly poured heather honey over multigrain loaf, then rich orchard fruits such as Comice pears and Red Delicious apples appear and add a fruity element to layers of peppery spice.

TASTE There is a peppered butter element to the nose that is extremely inviting. A toasted oak character reveals itself in the form of banana bread with custard and creamy brandy butter.

FINISH The spice builds on the palate, complemented by the slightly higher bottling strength, with allspice and lime cordial.

Comments

This is a distillery close to my heart, as it is the nearest distillery to my home town of Aberdeen. I have always found Glen Garioch's whiskies to be incredibly balanced and complex, offering fruit and spice in perfect proportions.

GLEN GARIOCH
1988 Whisky
Sponge Release

Single malt

PRICE ●●●●●

ABV 44.6%

NOSE   This was distilled before Glen Garioch changed their house style, so there is a beautiful floral peat smoke that carries this whisky. Banana, lime zest and slight menthol qualities fill the nose.

TASTE   Instantly there is a noticeably thick and luxurious texture on the palate, with beautiful tropical fruit notes of papaya and guava. The sweetness is fantastic and really welcoming.

FINISH   Direct and thick. The smoke is well integrated and carries waves of waxy fruitiness through the whisky.

Comments

Seeing an old Highland whisky presented like this is a real treat. The floral smoke element is a nod to a style of whisky that very few distilleries produce now. It is full and elegant, with sweet tropical fruit flavours derived from a single-refill hogshead cask.

Glenmorangie

Glenmorangie distillery is on the Dornoch Firth in Tain, Ross-shire, and was founded in 1843 by farmer William Matheson, although nowadays it is owned by French luxury conglomerate LVMH.

Glenmorangie's copper pot stills are the tallest in Scotland and famously stand as tall as an adult giraffe. The distillery is also renowned for its pioneering creativity in uniting tradition with innovation, and was one of the first to implement finishing casks, such as fortified and still wine casks, for its single malt. In 2020, Glenmorangie opened the doors to its new innovation distillery. The new 20-metre (66-foot) stillhouse can be seen for miles around and is aptly named The Lighthouse. Glenmorangie produces unpeated single malt and, for a limited time each year, also uses heavily roasted chocolate malt. This latter spirit features in the recipe for the premium bottling Glenmorangie Signet.

GLENMORANGIE
18 year old

Single malt

PRICE ●●●○○

ABV 43%

NOSE This whisky opens up with the classic distillery-driven character, showcasing crisp orange and creamy malt before more toasted and sugared mixed nut aromas develop.

TASTE Noticeably thick, resinous texture. The sherry influence is very apparent and definitely more so on the palate than the nose, with spiced almonds, vanilla and toffee brittle.

FINISH Long if not light, with dried fruit and fragrant vanilla.

Comments

Glenmorangie 18 year old is a great example of how clever cask selection can complement a gentle and light distillery character while adding much interest and complexity.

GLENMORANGIE
Signet

Single malt

PRICE ●●●●○

ABV 46%

NOSE Freshly brewed long coffee with a chocolate biscuit on the side. Spiced orange, cherries and honey make up a really intriguing nose.

TASTE The chocolate orange element of this dram dominates, but it is not overly sweet. This is due to the bitterness from the coffee note and creaminess from the specialised casks that have been used.

FINISH Creamy orange sponge pudding with a mocha sauce. This is long and unique as well as dessert-like and indulgent.

Comments

The Signet is a pioneer of heavily roasted barley use in Scotch whisky. This allows deeper and more intense cereal-driven flavours and presents an incredibly intelligent and visionary example of whisky from one of Scotland's most forward-thinking distilleries.

GLENMORANGIE
1997 Grand Vintage

Single malt

PRICE ●●●●●

ABV 43%

NOSE Intense floral notes with rose, jasmine and honeysuckle alongside red berries and buttery almond croissant.

TASTE Initially very zesty with some acidic pineapple, tart red berries and mandarin. There is spice as well, which is reminiscent of galangal and bitter almonds.

FINISH The finish is long, indulgent and has a really lovely big burst of orange oil and malt loaf.

Comments

Seeing slightly older Glenmorangie is always a treat. The spirit evolves from being light, soft and fresh to taking on a luxurious, almost oily character. This bottle is no different and certainly benefits from spending over half of the maturation in Château Montrose Bordeaux casks.

The Glenturret

The Glenturret is on the site of one of Scotland's oldest documented distilling locations, with records referencing production back as far as 1763, in the heart of Perthshire, near Crieff. It was acquired by a joint venture led by the Lalique Group and Swiss-American Hansjörg Wyss in 2019.

The restaurant at the distillery named The Glenturret Lalique was awarded a Michelin star in 2022, only seven months after opening, making The Glenturret the first whisky distillery ever to have received the prestigious award. In 2024 it was awarded a second Michelin star. This is not their only accolade: the distillery was also featured in the Guinness World Records thanks to their famous cat Towser, who is said to have captured 28,899 mice during her lifetime (1963–87), gaining her the title of the world's best mouse-catcher.

Both peated and unpeated whisky have been released from the distillery. Following the change of ownership, a new bottle design was presented for the core releases, while the more premium releases often come in exclusive Lalique decanters. The Glenturret releases annual batches of its core expressions that prominently feature sherry cask-matured spirit.

THE GLENTURRET
7 year old Peat Smoked 2023

Single malt

PRICE ●●○○○

ABV 46%

NOSE Fragrant vanilla incense, light oak and spiced Dundee marmalade.

TASTE The vanilla becomes the focal point of this whisky, with a taste reminiscent of apple strudel covered in cream.

FINISH The earthy and dry smoke is lingering and really complements the beautifully sweet notes.

Comments

I feel that bottling this whisky at seven years old is very clever. This allows the peat to be the main character, while The Glenturret's classic citrus and sweetness play the supporting role perfectly. A really great example of a whisky being exceptional at a younger age.

Royal Brackla

The Brackla distillery was founded in 1812 by Captain William Fraser and is located near Nairn in the Highlands. It sits on the Cawdor Estate, perhaps best known for being the setting for Shakespeare's *Macbeth*. The distillery was the first in Scotland to be granted a Royal Warrant in 1833 by King William IV as the chosen whisky for his court. The recognition earned the distillery its reputation as 'the King's own whisky', and also the new name Royal Brackla. The Royal Warrant was renewed by Queen Victoria in 1838, following her ascension to the throne. For many years, Royal Brackla was used for blending, but it has focused a little more on single malt releases since 2014. The range was revamped in 2019 with three core releases at 12, 18 and 21 years old. These whiskies are matured in first-fill sherry casks sourced from Spain, which give a rich and fruity style to the single malt.

ROYAL BRACKLA
12 year old

Single malt

PRICE ●●○○○

ABV 46%

NOSE Stewed apples and oranges mix with walnuts and buttered malt loaf.

TASTE Chocolate-coated peanuts, raisins and coffee cream alongside dried cherries and blackcurrant are all present, topped with burnt butter and brown sugar. This is a chewy whisky, showcasing some excellent influence from the finishing period in oloroso sherry.

FINISH The finish is rewarding with spiced oak, sugared (Jordan) almonds and sweet stewed fruit.

Comments

Since the rebrand in 2018, Royal Brackla has become a firm favourite among whisky drinkers. The use of first-fill oloroso sherry casks for this release adds a depth of flavour in the form of zingy citrus and winter spices, complementing Royal Brackla's fresh and fruity distillery character.

ROYAL BRACKLA
18 year old

Single malt

PRICE ●●●○○

ABV 46%

NOSE Pineapple cubes and retro confectionery are balanced with vanilla sponge and a slight hint of orange oil. A really juicy nose.

TASTE Peaches and apricots are prominent, with white chocolate and an almost lychee sweetness.

FINISH Long and sweet, with notes of coconut and barley sugar developing. The citrus is still present with amazing sweet orange notes coming through.

Comments

The new Royal Brackla whiskies using different sherry casks are a real testament to the influence these casks can bring. Using rare palo cortado casks, this whisky is incredibly fruity and showcases the softer side of the distillery's distillate, allowing the citrus and stone fruit qualities to be highlighted.

Tomatin

Tomatin can be found between Inverness and Aviemore in the Scottish Highlands, and its origins supposedly date back to the 15th century, although the first formal distillery was established in 1897. This only lasted a couple of years, most likely due to financial hardship, before production resumed again in 1909. Half of Tomatin's employees still live on site in the distillery houses, and the distillery has seen generations of families devote their entire working lives to the whisky production. The recession of the 1980s, however, saw the liquidation of Tomatin. Thankfully, in 1986 two Japanese companies, both counted among the distillery's best customers, bought the distillery so that it could reopen once again. Of those two saviours, Takara Shuzo remains as the majority shareholder to this day. Tomatin produces both unpeated and lightly peated spirit, the latter of which has been bottled under the name Cù Bòcan since 2013, a name that comes from the story of a ghostly dog that is said to have haunted the village of Tomatin. The peated spirit is produced every winter in limited batches, and just like the unpeated releases they frequently feature a variety of cask maturation types, from bourbon and sherry to red wine and port.

TOMATIN
14 year old

Single malt

PRICE ●●○○○

ABV 46%

NOSE Vanilla combines with red grapes and strawberries to provide an intensely fruity and sweet scent. There is some oak spice here as well.

TASTE More of the spice and tannin emerge, with cracked black pepper over dark chocolate strawberry sponge.

FINISH This is a concentrated if not rather short finish. It is straightforward and easy to understand. A delicious whisky showing great use of some of Portugal's best casks.

Comments

Tomatin has used port casks from some of Portugal's highest-quality wine producers to really highlight the fruitiness in the distillery character while adding fresh berries and wine-like sweetness to this excellent whisky.

TOMATIN
18 year old

Single malt

PRICE ●●●●○

ABV 46%

NOSE A thick nose of allspice, dark chocolate and cocoa-dusted almonds. Vanilla fudge, cinnamon butter and toffee apples add sweetness.

TASTE The palate continues thick and full-bodied, with dark honeycomb toffee and chocolate orange adding to the sweetness anticipated from the nose.

FINISH The finish on this sherry-influenced whisky is long and spicy with cinnamon, chilli and dark chocolate. It has a beautiful richness.

Comments

Over the past 10 years, this whisky has won fans and awards in equal measure, picking up no fewer than five major whisky awards, most recently Double Gold at the San Francisco World Spirits Competition in 2022. It is easy to see why: this is a fantastic whisky with excellent balance.

TOMATIN
36 year old Batch 11

Single malt

PRICE ● ● ● ● ●

ABV 45.1%

NOSE An immense aroma of grapefruit pith and Alphonso mango alongside vanilla and delicately toasted oak. Honeysuckle and elderflower add floral notes.

TASTE Sweet and full with more ripe, exotic fruit and heather honey. The freshness of this whisky at 36 years old is incredible. This is thick, viscous and mouth-coating.

FINISH The fruit builds with notes of peaches soaked in syrup and spices, with classic winter spice notes derived from sherry casks. The finish is long and there is almost a second burst of even more fruitiness after a couple of sips.

Comments

I first tasted this bottling in 2015 when the 36 year old was first released and found a flavour profile I had never encountered previously. Tomatin 36 year old is, and probably always will be, one of my fondest whisky-drinking experiences.

Aberlour

The first distillery in the village of Aberlour (pronounced 'a-buh-*lour*' as in 'our') in Speyside was built in the 1820s, but was later destroyed by a fire. The current distillery was built further up the River Spey by James Fleming in 1879 and was unfortunately also affected by a fire, but rebuilt once again. It still stands on the edge of Aberlour village, near the Linn Falls. After being acquired by French company Pernod Ricard in 1974, the whisky has gained a lot of popularity in France, one of the most important export markets for Scotch whisky. The distillery produces an unpeated spirit and is known for its sherried style of whisky, although some ex-bourbon-matured releases exist in the range as well. In 1997 the distillery released the first batch of the A'Bunadh expression, which has gained quite the cult following. This powerful, batch-strength whisky has been exclusively matured in first-fill sherry casks, without an age statement. A'Bunadh (pronounced 'a-*boon*-na') has proven to be a much-loved 'sherry bomb' among whisky drinkers.

ABERLOUR
A'Bunadh Batch 80

Single malt

PRICE ●●●○○

ABV 61%

NOSE An immense richness of toffee, cherries and chocolate in balance with sweet and fiery ginger.

TASTE Burnt orange and allspice coat the mouth with remarkable staying power, even with 61% alcohol. There is a sweetness reminiscent of rum and raisin ice cream.

FINISH Long finish with warmth from oloroso sherry casks adding spice and dried fruit sweetness.

Comments

Aberlour A'Bunadh is credited with popularising cask-strength first-fill sherry cask-matured Speyside whisky, and has paved the way for many distilleries to release their example of such a whisky. Through the 80-plus batches of A'Bunadh that have been released, one thing remains consistent: quality.

The Balvenie

The Balvenie was built by William Grant in 1892 and is still owned by the family company William Grant & Sons, which also operates the Glenfiddich and Kininvie malt distilleries located right next door in Dufftown, as well as the Girvan grain distillery in Ayrshire. The Balvenie distillery started production in May 1893, although the first official single malt release would not be available until 1971. The Balvenie is one of the few distilleries in Scotland that still operates traditional malting floors to malt a proportion of its own barley. The Balvenie also has its own cooperage (barrel making) on site, where many of the coopers have honed their craft for their entire careers. Although the distillery is primarily known for its unpeated whisky, it also runs peated spirit for one week every year and sources the peat from the local Speyside area. Former malt master David C Stewart was one of the pioneers in the 1980s to use the technique now known as 'wood finishing'. Stewart's creation, The Balvenie DoubleWood, is a fantastic example of this and was released in 1993 featuring maturation in both traditional casks and European oak sherry casks.

THE BALVENIE
12 year old
DoubleWood

Single malt

PRICE ●○○○○

ABV 40%

NOSE Extremely malty nose with cereal sweetness and honey-soaked granola; delicate fragrant oak and warm spiced cream.

TASTE There is a weight to The Balvenie whiskies and this expression perfectly showcases this. Honey is still present and the oak spice continues with some orange and soft ginger spice.

FINISH Spicy and dry with some lovely red apple notes developing on the finish. This is mid-length: not too long, not too short.

Comments

The Balvenie DoubleWood is a whisky classic. David Stewart, former malt master, pioneered the use of actively re-racking whisky in several casks to build up complex layers of flavours, a practice that has since become a crucial part of Scotch whisky making.

THE BALVENIE
21 year old
PortWood

Single malt

PRICE ●●●●○

ABV 40%

NOSE Raspberry jam on multigrain bread, white peach purée and a touch of fragrant smoke.

TASTE Complex, with immediate notes of dark cherry, chocolate and lighter raspberry or strawberry notes, then more delicate notes of sweetened almonds and cranberries dipped in white chocolate.

FINISH Long, lingering and spiced, with the sweetness of the port casks complementing the spice.

Comments

The Balvenie 21 year old is an incredibly luxurious whisky that uses the practice of finishing, which is at the heart of the majority of output from the distillery. This time, high-quality well-aged port casks from the Douro Valley in Portugal have been used to emphasise the fruity and rich spirit produced by rare craft at The Balvenie distillery.

THE BALVENIE
25 year old
Rare Marriages

Single malt

PRICE ●●●●●

ABV 48%

NOSE After 25 years in a combination of casks, this Balvenie is really mature, and has evolved into a very special whisky. Mellow traditional oak warmth, fragrant heather honey and caramelised orange peel.

TASTE Soft and subtle leather initially on the palate, with apple and pear pastry and hints of toasted meringue.

FINISH The indulgent sweetness lasts a remarkably long time, and the tannin from the sherry cask is the real highlight.

Comments

The Rare Marriages is a relatively new series from The Balvenie distillery.

Benriach

Benriach (pronounced 'ben-*ree*-ach') distillery was established on the old Riach farm in Speyside in 1898 by founder John Duff. Unfortunately, the distillery was only in operation for a couple of years before having to shut down after an industry-wide collapse in whisky prices. Benriach would not produce any whisky again until 1965, but thankfully the distillery was saved by its floor maltings, which supplied malted barley for the nearby Longmorn distillery. Once whisky production resumed, Benriach soon began exploring the use of peated malt for its spirit, something that had been traditional in the Speyside region but was becoming increasingly uncommon. Today, of course, Speyside is known for its unpeated whiskies. However, this was not the only style of spirit that Benriach would add to its portfolio. In the 1990s, production began of the first batches of a triple-distilled spirit. Today, the distillery creates three different spirit styles: double-distilled unpeated, double-distilled peated and triple-distilled unpeated. The traditional malting floors opened up once more in 2012, after being decommissioned at the end of the 20th century, and are now being used for limited production each year.

BENRIACH
The Sixteen

Single malt

PRICE ●●○○○

ABV 43%

NOSE Creamy and nutty praline with slightly burnt honey. There is also a hint of orchard fruit reminiscent of apple pie with vanilla ice cream.

TASTE The sweet, spiced stewed apple and pear flavours continue, with a delicious toasted oak character providing a slight dry smoke. Caramel on the palate delivers more sweetness to counter the smoke.

FINISH Sweet and toasted almonds caramelised in sugar dominates the palate, with a touch of creamy vanilla and warm allspice.

Comments

The Sixteen was released in 2023, and was the latest to join Benriach's core releases in their new presentation. It perfectly showcases the skill of blending peated and unpeated whisky to create a succinct and flavourful expression.

BENRIACH
The Twenty Five

Single malt

PRICE ●●●●○

ABV 46%

NOSE Rich smoked apricot with spiced toffee and warm brandy butter served to accompany it.

TASTE The sweetness provided by vanilla, cinnamon-dusted apples and caramel intertwines elegantly with mature smoke reminiscent of bonfire embers; soft, subtle but definitely still present.

FINISH The spice really ramps up on the finish and a lot more of the Madeira cask influence is revealed. Rich baked fruit and warming caramel spice leave a long finish.

Comments

The Twenty Five marries elegant, soft smoke with rich, dessert-like sweetness to create a whisky that showcases a more traditional side of Speyside.

BENRIACH
The Thirty

Single malt

PRICE ●●●●●

ABV 46%

NOSE Intense fruit verging on fresh blackberries and blackcurrants, assisted by an incredibly subtle smoke, almost from a fire in the distance.

TASTE Redcurrants and marzipan are the primary tastes here, backed up by soft brown sugar-coated pastry and rich honey.

FINISH The fruit turns more preserved and the sugar more caramelised. The wood smoke fades to a whisper and helps carry the waves of red berries provided by the port casks.

Comments

The Benriach distillery is home to some of the oldest peated whisky on the River Spey. Such whisky is so rare that seeing releases like this are refreshing. The composition of Speyside peat is different from that of other, more maritime locations, and a more floral and dry smoke is present.

Benromach

Benromach distillery was originally built in 1898 and went through a long period of being shut down and reopened by different owners due to various economic factors. In 1993, the shell of the distillery was taken over by the family-owned whisky company Gordon & MacPhail, who brought it back to life. It took the company five years of careful renovation and the installation of new distilling equipment to get the distillery ready for whisky making again, and production finally recommenced in 1998. Benromach is located in the Speyside area of Forres, Moray, and primarily produces a lightly peated spirit, as the Urquhart family at Gordon & MacPhail was keen to bring back the 'lost' historic style of Speyside whiskies. In 2020 Benromach launched its rebranding, which featured a new look inspired by the distillery's history. The redesign took inspiration from the hand-painted sign that used to decorate the roof over the kiln, as well as the distinctive red brick chimney and red doors that can be found around the distillery.

BENROMACH
15 year old

Single malt

PRICE ●●○○○

ABV 43%

NOSE Sherry and vanilla work in harmony in this whisky, offering orange peel, gingerbread and earthy peat smoke.

TASTE A delightful palate of rich fruit cake, eucalyptus and ripe navel oranges alongside sweet notes of milk chocolate-covered almonds.

FINISH The fruit cake is still present, this time with more buttery notes and a creamy, sweet coffee.

Comments

Benromach is a fascinating distillery with a small production team that takes pride in making whisky by hand and not relying on computers and automation. A sip of this expression conjures images of these more traditional distilleries.

BENROMACH
21 year old

Single malt

PRICE ●●●●○

ABV 43%

NOSE Fresh raspberry, toasted oats and sweet, light honey. This is almost reminiscent of cranachan made with a softly peated whisky.

TASTE Rich and spiced dark chocolate with more fresh fruit. Orange is added to the notes of raspberry and complements the spice provided by the sherry casks used in this expression.

FINISH The smoke is sweet and fragrant, and works well with the fruity flavours of orange and raspberry found on the palate.

Comments

Benromach's medium-bodied spirit is suitable for various lengths of maturation, and I find this 21-year-old incredible for portraying the traditional style of lost Speyside distilleries. Soft and subtle smoke becomes much more integrated after 21 years of maturation.

Craigellachie

Craigellachie (pronounced 'cray-*gell*-ack-ee') is located in Speyside, and is renowned for its sulphuric spirit stemming from the use of worm-tub condensers. The name 'worm tub' describes the condenser design well, as it consists of a long, coiled, worm-like copper pipe that is submersed in a big vat, or tub, of water. Nowadays, very few distilleries use traditional worm-tub condensers, as the more modern shell and tube condensers provide increased copper contact, which tends to result in a lighter style of spirit with less sulphurous aromas. However, some sulphuric flavours can be desirable, and certain Scottish distilleries like Craigellachie embrace this heavier character. The spirit is often described as 'robust' with notes of tropical pineapple and, when it is younger, a whiff of struck match. The distillery was built in 1890, designed by famed distillery architect Charles Chree Doig. Locally, it was known as the White Horse distillery for some time, on account of its ownership by Peter Mackie, of distiller and blender White Horse, and Alexander Edward. It is therefore unsurprising that Craigellachie was a core component of the famous White Horse blended Scotch. When Edward left in 1900 to pursue other ventures, the distillery was left in the hands of White Horse Distillers. In 1998, Craigellachie was bought by Bacardi and is today part of the John Dewar & Sons portfolio. In 2014, a range of Craigellachie single malts was launched in earnest.

CRAIGELLACHIE
13 year old

Single malt

PRICE ●○○○○

ABV 46%

NOSE Baked apples and beeswax are both initially obvious on the nose; barbecued sweetcorn and slightly burnt sugar then develop.

TASTE Barley sugar and creamy malt coat the palate and then there is a fresh, zingy note of sweet pineapple followed by pistachio.

FINISH Malt biscuits and more baked apples leave a thick coating on the finish.

Comments

The texture and viscosity of Craigellachie whiskies always stand out to me. They are rich, generous and often slightly dry. This core expression is one of the best whiskies in the world at showcasing how old-fashioned condensers can make a heavy spirit.

CRAIGELLACHIE
23 year old

Single malt

PRICE ●●●●○

ABV 46%

NOSE Immensely tropical, with notes of lime and pineapple on the initial nose. Toasted oak and golden syrup emerge.

TASTE The golden syrup develops into salted caramel and is joined by clove-studded orange zest and a dusting of cinnamon over bran flakes.

FINISH Craigellachie's classic sulphured reputation is apparent here, but it is kept at bay after 23 years in cask. It presents itself as a pleasant spice and leads to a long finish.

Comments

The waxiness really does complement what I would describe as a very cereal-forward whisky. I really love the way Craigellachie ages; it becomes less about the cask influence and more about the inherent fruit of the spirit produced at the distillery.

Dailuaine

Dailuaine (pronounced 'dal-*you*-in') was built in 1852 by the farmer William Mackenzie and sits near the foot of Ben Rinnes in Speyside. In Scottish Gaelic *dail uaine* means 'green valley' and is named after the elegant undulations of the Spey Valley where the distillery is located. The distillery was the biggest Speyside single malt distillery at the end of the 19th century. It is rare to find single malt bottlings of Dailuaine, as the distillery only releases a small amount. Single malt releases can most commonly be found through the Diageo Flora & Fauna range, as a 16-year-old sherry-matured expression, or occasionally as Manager's Drams. Each of the expressions in the Flora & Fauna collection is represented by an animal, and the Dailuaine label is decorated by a badger. Most of the spirit produced at Dailuaine is used in the blending of whiskies for the Johnnie Walker range. The spirit is filled at the Cambus site and then transported to Blackgrange Bond for maturation in the Diageo-owned warehouses.

DAILUAINE
16 year old
Flora & Fauna

Single malt

PRICE ●●○○○

ABV 43%

NOSE A sweetness is provided by peanut brittle topped with dark cocoa powder. The nuttiness is definitely dominant and transitions to a toasted almond note.

TASTE The richness and almost meaty quality is first observed with rich gamey notes, almost like a dark chocolate and venison sauce, then with bitter orange and lemon providing some freshness.

FINISH Spice and sweetness are there in perfect balance with notes of almonds tossed in orange sugar and a faint hint of wood smoke.

Comments

The Dailuaine Flora & Fauna has long been a go-to for fans of the now-discontinued Mortlach bottling of the same series. It is easy to see why, with the two whiskies sharing that rich, meaty quality that has made Mortlach so desired over the past decade.

GlenAllachie

GlenAllachie is one of Scotland's few independently owned and managed distilleries, having been acquired in 2017 by Billy Walker, Graham Stevenson and Trisha Savage. Master distiller Billy Walker, who has over 50 years of experience in the whisky industry, runs this Speyside distillery nestled at the foot of Ben Rinnes. The distillery puts a lot of effort into its wood policy, which includes a wide variety of cask types, and 2023 saw GlenAllachie spend £2.7 million on casks alone. Over 50,000 casks are held in 16 on-site warehouses waiting to be used for one of the bottlings from the distillery. The new owners have chosen to reduce annual production capacity from 4 million litres (1 million US gallons) to around 800,000 (200,000 US gallons) litres of alcohol to prioritise quality over quantity. The distillery has also increased the fermentation period to 160 hours to encourage an ester-rich and fruity spirit. In 2018, GlenAllachie started producing peated spirit for the first time and recently began releasing this smoky whisky under its own brand, which so far includes four core releases.

THE GLENALLACHIE
15 year old

Single malt

PRICE ●●○○○

ABV 46%

NOSE Dark chocolate and hazelnut ice cream with rich toffee and date sauce. The nose is immediately very inviting and sweet.

TASTE The rich and dessert-like notes continue on the palate, with fresh ginger, cinnamon and the zingy spice of cardamom – all adding character.

FINISH Strong coffee with a hint of rose oil and salted caramel complete this incredibly indulgent whisky.

Comments

When Billy Walker bought GlenAllachie in 2017 he inherited a swathe of casks, and it is credit to his meticulous whisky making that we see, time after time, quality releases from his warehouses.

Glenfarclas

Glenfarclas distillery in Speyside has been owned by the same family for five generations. John Grant famously bought the distillery farm, located by the foot of Ben Rinnes, in 1865 for 511 pounds and 19 shillings. The name comes from the Scottish Gaelic for 'valley of the green grass'. John and George, grandchildren of founder John, continued the distillery business and went on to form the J & G Grant company, which remains the owner of Glenfarclas. The distillery increased production due to the high demand from blenders during the mid 1900s. However, as demand started decreasing by the late 1960s, George made the decision to prioritise laying down stock for the distillery's own bottlings. Thanks to this and his determination not to sell all of the spirit as blending stock, Glenfarclas has an impressive collection of aged stock today, dating back to at least the 1950s. Today, these rare spirits are bottled as part of the Family Casks collection. Glenfarclas is one of few distilleries that still use the traditional method of directly firing the stills, as opposed to the indirect steam heating that is more common nowadays. The traditional distillation helps create the unique Glenfarclas spirit, which is typically matured in sherry casks.

GLENFARCLAS
15 year old

Single malt

PRICE ●●○○○

ABV 46%

NOSE Immediate notes of sherry come through on the nose alongside rum-soaked raisins, oily walnuts and a slight earthy quality.

TASTE Raisins are still prominent, and fresh orange oil with a touch of almond begins to emerge. There is also a light drizzle of milk chocolate.

FINISH The finish is long, with waves of that brilliant walnut and orange oil continuing to develop.

Comments

This whisky really does grab the attention of whisky drinkers all over the world. It is old-school, sherry oak matured and representative of a style of whisky that is not only famous for the region but also intrinsically linked to the house style of the distillery.

GLENFARCLAS
30 year old

Single malt

PRICE ●●●●●

ABV 43%

NOSE Dark and almost smoked, reminiscent of an old Pedro Ximénez sherry, showcasing coffee, candied peels and black treacle (blackstrap molasses).

TASTE The thickness of this whisky is immediately noticeable; it is spicy and sweet with more citrus peels and raisins baked in pastry.

FINISH Long and lingering with notes of rubber and damp oak.

Comments

The Glenfarclas 30 year old, for me, is a real treat and still represents unbelievable value for money when searching for aged malts. I adore how well integrated the oak has become in this whisky over the three decades of maturation in classic dunnage-style warehouses.

Glenfiddich

In the summer of 1886, William Grant broke ground in the construction of Glenfiddich distillery, with a little help from his two daughters and seven sons. The following year, the distillery was finished and, on Christmas Day 1887, distillation commenced. Throughout its history, Glenfiddich has been passed down through the generations and is still run by family-owned William Grant & Sons. Glenfiddich's owners increased production in the 1920s, at the height of Prohibition in the USA, when other producers were suffering from a slump in export sales. This meant the company was well placed to supply aged stock to a thirsty public after Prohibition's repeal. At the end of the 1950s, the company appointed a resident coppersmith to service the family's distilleries and, not long after, built a dedicated cooperage, thereby preserving two historic arts vital to whisky production. The iconic triangular bottle was designed by Hans Schleger in 1961, inspired by the trinity of ingredients that makes Glenfiddich: water, yeast and malted barley. Glenfiddich's whiskies are carefully put together by malt master Brian Kinsman, although sometimes expressions are created out of the unexpected. In 2010 there was extreme snowfall in Speyside, which caused one of the Glenfiddich warehouse roofs to collapse. The team worked around the clock to save as many of the exposed casks as possible, and later bottled their contents as Glenfiddich Snow Phoenix.

GLENFIDDICH
12 year old

Single malt

PRICE ●○○○○

ABV 40%

NOSE Pear drops, elderflower and toasted oak are all present on the nose. This is a delicate whisky with some very soft vanilla.

TASTE The vanilla really shines here and mingles with further notes of pear, this time freshly cut fruit, and apples. The cereal is prominent as well, with honey-soaked oats and malt.

FINISH There is delicate spice, but mostly a light sweetness reminiscent of a summer cocktail with touches of elderflower and pear.

Comments

When Charles and Sandy Gordon started selling Glenfiddich single malt commercially, the world of whisky changed. This gave focus to the place and the people creating the spirits. This whisky offers all of that: it is the very taste of summer afternoons in Speyside. The 12-year-old is consistent and, in my view, deserves a place on any whisky shelf.

GLENFIDDICH
21 year old
Gran Reserva
Rum Cask Finish

Single malt

PRICE ●●●●○

ABV 40%

NOSE A rich nose of dark manuka honey, heavy vanilla and orange peel. There is some spice in the form of cloves and a touch of cinnamon.

TASTE The rich vanilla continues and becomes somewhat buttery; think crème brûlée. The spice is still there, with cloves becoming most prominent.

FINISH The finish of this whisky is very long, especially for the conservative strength. Notes of Dundee marmalade and mocha coffee.

Comments

Glenfiddich 21 year old has gone through various different names and livery changes, but this whisky remains in my top five of all time. This may be the memories associated with drinking it or indeed the way the whisky suits my palate. What I do know is that every time I have a glass of this, a smile is seen across my face.

GLENFIDDICH
30 year old
Suspended Time

Single malt

PRICE ● ● ● ● ●

ABV 43%

NOSE After 30 years' maturing, there is a freshness to this whisky in the form of strawberry and raspberry sponge soaked with crème de fraise. Very light and very delicate.

TASTE The lightness and subtlety continue, with notes of lemon cheesecake and just a touch of cinnamon-spiked apple ice cream.

FINISH The sweetness builds and builds, and it is on the finish that we fully see the beauty of the added spice, this time with just a hint of white pepper.

Comments

Glenfiddich is a distillery that, for me, is capable of maintaining a distillery character over a wide range of ages. This whisky showcases the classic distillery notes of apple and soft fruits.

The Glenlivet

The story goes that, in August 1822, King George IV arrived in Scotland for a state visit, and such was the reputation of the whisky produced in and around Morayshire's Livet valley, he was served a glass of Glenlivet malt whisky. Almost certainly untaxed, it would no doubt have been considered contraband at the time. Two years later, after the implementation of the Excise Act of 1823, George Smith of Upper Drumin Farm famously became the first licensed distiller in the parish of Glenlivet. Smith's Glenlivet was a roaring success, so much so that he built a new, larger distillery nearby at Minmore in the late 1850s. In the following years Glenlivet's reputation grew, and many other distilleries tried to profit from the Glenlivet name, adding the word as a suffix to their own. By the end of the 19th century there was a host of distilleries trading off the name, such as 'Aberlour-Glenlivet', 'Tamdhu-Glenlivet' and so on, which weren't located in the Livet valley, even by the most lenient definition. In many ways, the name can be thought of as a precursor to the whisky region of Speyside, and it led to the joke that the Livet valley was the longest in Scotland. John's son George fought hard against this and in 1884 secured the rights for Glenlivet to be known as 'The' Glenlivet, thereby establishing the Smith's distillery as the one and only, alhough it didn't stop others from using the suffix. Today owned by Chivas Brothers, a subsidiary of Pernod Ricard, The Glenlivet is the oldest legal distillery in Scotland, having operated almost continuously since 1824, and produces one of the world's most popular single malts. It has an impressive capacity of 21 million litres (5.5 million US gallons) per year, making it one of the biggest single malt distilleries in Scotland.

THE GLENLIVET
18 year old

Single malt

PRICE ●●●○○

ABV 40%

NOSE A well-rounded nose of honey, barley sugar and chewy citrus peels. The sweetness builds into toffee and sweetened cereal notes, with a tiny influence of wood smoke.

TASTE The orchard fruits jump out here, with notes of apple crumble and bread and butter pudding. There is almost a menthol edge with a tiny bit of fresh mint.

FINISH The finish dries out and the sherried notes of this whisky start to dominate. There are notes of soft sultanas and raisins and a slight, pleasant bitterness from the oak.

Comments

The Glenlivet 18 year old is a fantastic expression from the first registered distillery in Scotland. The balance and softness of this whisky perfectly suit the valley the distillery calls home.

THE GLENLIVET
25 year old

Single malt

PRICE ●●●●●

ABV 43%

NOSE Rich notes of blackberry and bramble jam with a hint of soft vanilla. The longer this whisky is in the glass, the more fragrant heather honey starts to present itself.

TASTE Rich and sweet with more wild berries. The oak element here really balances and adds richness to this whisky.

FINISH The sweetness builds on the finish with milk chocolate and toffee. The spice derived from the oak also develops.

Comments

The use of Tronçais oak Cognac casks to finish this whisky has added a lovely fragrant sweetness, and when paired with more traditional Pedro Ximénez casks, creates a beautifully balanced and intriguing whisky.

The Glenrothes

The Glenrothes (pronounced 'glen-*roth*-iss') was established in 1879 in the
Speyside town of Rothes. From the beginning, the distillery's whisky was a
popular component for blending and was used in well-known names such as
Cutty Sark and the Famous Grouse. In 1987, the established relationship with
the Cutty Sark blends brought The Glenrothes into the portfolio of London wine
and spirit retailers Berry Bros. & Rudd, which owned half the Cutty Sark brand
at that time. Alhough The Glenrothes spirit was still used predominantly for
blends, single malt bottlings started being released in 1993. Unusually, these
first releases were vintages, rather than the more recognisable age statements,
as a nod to Berry Bros. & Rudd's link to the wine trade. The Edrington Group
and William Grant & Sons acquired the distillery in 1999 as part of the group's
purchase of Highland Distillers, but Berry Bros. bought the Glenrothes brand in
exchange for Cutty Sark in 2010. During this time, Edrington still had ownership
of the distillery and supplied Berry Bros. with spirit. The Glenrothes brand was
bought back by Edrington seven years later, once more uniting the brand and the
distillery, and the following year a repackaging of the range was announced. The
rebrand saw the end of the vintage releases the distillery had become known for,
replaced by more conventional age statements.

THE GLENROTHES
18 year old

Single malt

PRICE ●●●●○

ABV 43%

NOSE Initially this whisky is reminiscent of a French patisserie, with notes of toasted almonds, cherry and candied orange.

TASTE Dried citrus and stone fruits develop, with spice provided by fresh ginger, finally joined by dark chocolate.

FINISH Long, spicy and sweet. This is a beautifully rich example of a well-aged sherry cask-matured expression, carrying the classic notes of dark chocolate and spice through the nose, taste and finish.

Comments

Launched as part of The Glenrothes' Soleo Collection, named after the process of sun-drying grapes for the production of wine. We therefore expect lots of those beautiful rich European oak influences to come through, and this does not disappoint.

THE GLENROTHES
25 year old

Single malt

PRICE ●●●●●

ABV 43%

NOSE Tropical fruits like pineapple and mango are present on the initial nose, turning to charred pineapple over time.

TASTE Fragrant wood notes of pine resin and salted caramel make the palate very luxurious, while a floral note starts to develop.

FINISH The floral notes become prominent with honeysuckle and dried mandarin. Very clean and lingering.

Comments

The Glenrothes 25 year old is predominantly matured in first-fill sherry-seasoned casks, which give the spirit the opportunity to become deep, rich and spicy. However, this particular example has maintained some freshness and lingering sweetness that is unexpected yet intriguing.

Glen Grant

The small town of Rothes in Speyside is where the Glen Grant distillery was established in 1840 by the brothers James and John Grant, the former also the founder of the Morayshire Railway Company. The business was inherited by James's nephew, also called James Grant, but affectionately known as 'the Major'. In 1872 he went on to create a 22-acre Victorian garden at the distillery, replete with overflowing greenhouses. This 'garden of splendours' was the only distillery garden of its kind in Scotland, and was inspired by James's travels and samples of exotic plants and fruits from around the world. James also introduced Glen Grant's tall and slender stills along with the purifier that defines the style of single malt still created today. Thanks to him, the distillery is also known for being the first to have electric light, which was installed around the town as well. After the Major passed away in 1931, the distillery was inherited by his grandson, Douglas MacKessack. In 1946, Dennis Malcolm was born on the distillery site and in 1961 he was employed by MacKessack in the distillery's cooperage, becoming the third generation in his family to work at the distillery. Through changes of ownership from private hands to Allied, and then to present owners Campari Group, Dennis Malcolm remained involved with the distillery near constantly throughout the five decades of his career. After acquiring the distillery in 2006, Campari Group appointed Dennis Malcolm as master distiller. Today he is one of the longest-serving distillers in Scotland, with over 60 years' experience in the industry.

GLEN GRANT
18 year old

Single malt

PRICE ●●●●○

ABV 43%

NOSE Notes of elderflower, lemon drops and fresh papaya. This is a very fruit-forward whisky with a delicate and inviting aroma.

TASTE Light caramel develops on the palate with notes of lemon sponge soaked in vanilla custard.

FINISH Spice starts to develop, with soft notes of almonds tossed in sugar and baking spice, and a fresh creamy finish completes this whisky.

Comments

I have found that all Glen Grant whiskies display a signature softness and sweetness, and this 18-year-old is no different. Matured exclusively in ex-American oak casks, the canvas of light spirit produced at Glen Grant lends itself well to the influence of such casks.

GLEN GRANT
21 year old

Single malt

PRICE ●●●●○

ABV 46%

NOSE Light blossom honey and juicy orchard fruits, such as Comice pears and Braeburn apples.

TASTE Initially this is a very creamy malt with notes of soft vanilla. Sweet apricot jam and toasted, spiced pineapple add complexity.

FINISH More vanilla is present, with toasted coconut and zingy tropical fruit.

Comments

The 21-year-old was released in 2023 and begins a journey by the owners to elevate the offering of Glen Grant to premium level. There is some sherry cask influence in this whisky, which adds depth to what is usually a very light style of whisky.

Glen Moray

Glen Moray started out as the Elgin West Brewery in the 1830s before being transformed into a distillery. The first spirit was distilled at this new Speyside distillery in September 1897. During the First World War it fell silent, before being purchased by the wine and spirits merchants Macdonald & Muir. Throughout the 1950s, the distillery was expanded and updated to double its output and later, in 1987, production increased to seven days a week. At the end of the 20th century, Glen Moray launched its first wood-'mellowed' whiskies (before the term 'finishing' had been coined) and was among the first to use white wine casks, especially those that previously held Chardonnay, for single malt whisky. The distillery has continued exploring the influence of a wide variety of different casks and the use of table- and fortified-wine casks has become Glen Moray's hallmark. In 2023 the Glen Moray Explorer range was introduced, which, alongside Our Classic and peated Smoky Classic, features double-cask whiskies finished in casks that previously held sherry, Cabernet Sauvignon, Chardonnay, Shiraz and port wines.

GLEN MORAY
18 year old

Single malt

PRICE ●●○○○

ABV 47.2%

NOSE Freshly picked plums drizzled in rich caramel and allspice. There is a spicy character from the oak, which adds dryness.

TASTE Floral and mellow with notes of woodruff and white chocolate, vanilla and fresh orange zest.

FINISH Soft and straightforward with plum compote on multi-seed toast.

Comments

Glen Moray is a distillery that has a wide portfolio of finished whiskies. This expression, however, is fully matured in first-fill bourbon casks, allowing the sweet and soft distillery character to be fully expressed.

GLEN MORAY
21 year old
Portwood Finish

Single malt

PRICE ●●●●○

ABV 46.3%

NOSE Wild strawberry and ginger jam with all-butter shortbread and tuile biscuits. A very fruity nose showcasing all of the beauty of cask finishing.

TASTE Notes of Black Forest gâteau and aniseed (anise) initially, then heat from cracked black pepper and mild chilli.

FINISH Salted caramel and strawberries covered in chocolate. This whisky leaves a sweetness on the finish that helps balance the spice found on the palate.

Comments

Finishing this whisky in port casks has added a freshness in the form of red berries that works so beautifully with the light and soft spirit of Glen Moray.

Longmorn

John Duff had already worked at The GlenDronach and founded Glenlossie when he travelled abroad to try his luck in South Africa and America. Things did not go to plan, and upon his return to Scotland he shifted his focus and first built Longmorn distillery in 1893, before setting up another a stone's throw away – Benriach – outside the Speyside capital of Elgin. Longmorn's spirit was being used in blends such as VAT 69 and Dewar's at the start of the next century, and is still primarily used for blending. For a short period of time in the 1920s, a young Japanese chemist and businessman by the name of Masataka Taketsuru worked at the distillery during his stay in Scotland. Once he returned to his home country, he became known as one of the fathers of Japanese whisky, and later founded the Japanese distiller Nikka. It is for this reason that the stills at Nikka's Yoichi distillery are said to have been modelled on those at Longmorn. Very few single malt releases can be found from Longmorn. In 2007, a 16-year-old release was launched and it can also be found as part of the Distillery Reserve or Secret Speyside collections from Chivas Brothers, the blender that owns the distillery today.

LONGMORN
18 year old

Single malt

PRICE ●●●●○

ABV 57.6%

NOSE Rich cacao with buttery caramel and an exotic fruit salad of mango, pineapple and coconut.

TASTE The coconut comes through stronger and complements some soft apricot and more sweetness from the toffee and caramel.

FINISH The alcohol carries this finish. There is more fresh mango and sugared (Jordan) almonds.

Comments

Longmorn has often been described as the 'blender's secret' because it is such a versatile spirit that works well in a range of casks. Here we see an American oak-matured expression revealing the lighter and fruity side of the distillery.

LONGMORN
22 year old

Single malt

PRICE ●●●●●

ABV 54.5%

NOSE Fruit driven with notes of freshly cut white peach and Victoria plum, before some spice from cinnamon and nutmeg start to appear.

TASTE Sweet and juicy tangerine, rhubarb and apple chutney all mingle to create a very complex yet delicate whisky.

FINISH Long and sweet with the softness of a beautifully prepared peach Melba dessert served with coconut ice cream.

Comments

Longmorn, for me, is a distillery that works so beautifully at this sort of age. I often find sweetness that reminds me of traditional confectionery and fruit salad. This expression is no different.

The Macallan

The Macallan distillery is located on the Macallan estate near Craigellachie in Speyside. The distillery was founded by Alexander Reid, who obtained his licence to distil in 1824. Traditionally the whisky from the distillery was used for blends like Famous Grouse, but The Macallan has grown to become one of the most well-known single malt brands in the world today. Famed for its predominant use of sherry casks, The Macallan rose to prominence off the back of now-legendary bottlings like the 1926 Valerio Adami 60 years old, which holds the record for the largest sum ever paid for a bottle of whisky: £2.1 million. The brand is not only recognisable as a common sight on whisky shelves; The Macallan also has a history of appearing in films since the 1970s, the best-known instances being in the James Bond films *Skyfall* and *Spectre*. Following the creation of its brand-new distillery, which launched in 2018, it is now also one of the largest in Scotland. It was designed by internationally acclaimed architects Rogers Stirk Harbour + Partners and its distinctive 'rolling' concept was inspired by the surrounding Scottish landscape. The single malt spirit from The Macallan tends to be matured in American or European sherry-seasoned casks, and to secure this supply it recently purchased a 50 per cent stake in sherry winemaker Bodegas Grupo Estévez SL and wholly acquired its long-time cask supplier, the cooperage Vasyma.

THE MACALLAN
12 year old
Sherry Oak Cask

Single malt

PRICE ●●●○○

ABV 40%

NOSE Rich, oily and full. There are notes of raisins soaked in Calvados, waxy walnuts and a floral note of meadowsweet.

TASTE Bitter orange marmalade and citrus peels coated in sugar. There are also notes of chocolate pastry and a spice builds from ginger.

FINISH Long and mouth-coating, the richness from the chocolate and ginger really shines through.

Comments

The Macallan distillery continues to produce really identifiable whiskies thanks to the thick and rich feel of the liquid on the palate. It is testament to the commitment that goes into sourcing only the best wood to mature their whisky in.

THE MACALLAN
18 year old
Sherry Oak Cask

Single malt

PRICE ●●●●○

ABV 43%

NOSE Treacle tart with spiced orange sorbet on the side. The rich notes of caramelised sugar are most apparent. Dark chocolate and subtle softened cherries start to come through.

TASTE Softened dates dipped in dark chocolate. Ginger snaps and sweet vanilla all intertwine to create beautiful harmony.

FINISH Lingering with oak-derived spice, mixed dried fruit and oily walnuts.

Comments

After 18 years in European oak sherry casks, this whisky has developed rich, complex and balanced flavours. For me, it harks back to a time of amazing integration of spirit character and cask influence: a beautiful example of allowing both to work in perfect unison.

THE MACALLAN
30 year old
Sherry Oak Cask

Single malt

PRICE ●●●●●

ABV 43%

NOSE A nose reminiscent of a Middle Eastern market, with spices and fruit in abundance. Cinnamon, star anise and mild chilli all play their part.

TASTE Dark chocolate with freshly pressed orange oil, stem (preserved) ginger and gently toasted oak. There is a dense note of baked filo pastry, almost caramelised with honey and spices.

FINISH Rich with spice, more orange oil and well-fed Christmas cake. The density of this whisky ensures a very long and lingering finish.

Comments

The Macallan Sherry Oak 30 year old is evidence of the patience required to leave a spirit undisturbed and allow that spirit to converse with the cask. After 30 years it is direct and precise.

Tamdhu

Tamdhu distillery has been producing single malt in Speyside since 1897. Records show that within its opening year the distillery had already acquired its first shipment of sherry casks. A group of like-minded entrepreneurs raised the equivalent to what would have been £20 million today to build the distillery, and also enlisted distillery architect Charles Chree Doig to design what was considered to be a modern, even innovative distillery. Tamdhu was silent between 1911–13 and again between 1927–48, but survived and was even expanded in the 1970s. In 2009 the distillery was forced to close its doors, but was reopened a mere two years later by Ian Macleod Distillers. The new owners are dedicated to sherry cask maturation and decided to mature all Tamdhu spirit destined to be bottled as single malt exclusively in American and European sherry casks, while spirit used for blending is still filled into other cask types, commonly ex-bourbon barrels.

TAMDHU
15 year old

Single malt

PRICE ●●●○○

ABV 46%

NOSE Charred orange zest and toasted cereal work with fruit slice thickly spread with salted butter. It is an inviting nose with lots of beautiful soft spice and rich sweetness.

TASTE Dried apricot and cherries mixed with notes of vanilla fudge and wood polish. The depth of the fudge notes is particularly noticeable.

FINISH The malt is the star of the show here, with more fudge and thick, oily citrus peels creating the perfect balance of cereal sweetness and fruit.

Comments

I find this whisky an excellent example of how to ensure a spirit is not dominated by cask: although the influence of the sherry casks is apparent, even pronounced, the spirit of Tamdhu does not get lost.

TAMDHU
18 year old

Single malt

PRICE ●●●●○

ABV 46.8%

NOSE Initially there are sharp cherries and baked plums, turning sweeter over time, with fruit and nut chocolate and honeyed porridge (oatmeal).

TASTE Freshly baked apple and raisin pie come through on the palate with a touch of vanilla ice cream to add creaminess.

FINISH A long finish, with notes of cooked apple and classic notes of oloroso sherry adding spice and nuttiness.

Comments

While Tamdhu has produced fine whiskies for over a century now, this recent addition to the core releases has been welcomed by fans of sherry cask-matured whiskies, as it adds more power and richness to the 15-year-old from the same distillery, while maintaining the classic notes of oily nuts and dark chocolate that high-quality casks can give a whisky over time.

Highland Park

Highland Park distillery was founded in Kirkwall on the island of Orkney in 1798, but would not get its licence until nearly 30 years later. The location, at a latitude of 58.9847°N, is exposed to the elements: winds can reach up to 100mph in winter and the distillery is one of only two that currently produces whisky on the island. Because of the climate there are very few trees on Orkney, but plenty of heather, which contributes to the unique peat the distillery uses for its production. The distillery is notable for producing a small proportion of its peated malt in traditional floor maltings on site, using peat sourced from Hobbister Moor, approximately 7 miles from the distillery. Orkney is known for its Norse heritage, as the island was invaded in the ninth century and ruled by the Vikings until 1468. The Norse influence is still evident on the island, in buildings and culture as well as the Highland Park branding, which is a nod to this heritage. The core range features whiskies such as the 12-year-old Viking Honour and the 18-year-old Viking Pride, both of which are bottled in the distinctive Highland Park bottle with embossed glass inspired by the ornate wood carving in the ancient *stavkirke* (wooden stave church) in Urnes, Norway.

HIGHLAND PARK
18 year old Viking Pride

Single malt

PRICE ●●●●○

ABV 43%

NOSE Heather honey and marzipan present themselves first, with some richer cherries and light toffee coming across over time.

TASTE A note of freshly brewed espresso starts to appear, with thick cream on the side. This is a complex palate with some allspice coming through as well. Think sweetened Turkish coffee.

FINISH The finish is long, spiced and indulgent with notes of heather, Brazil nut and a touch of light mint.

Comments

The Highland Park 18 year old was introduced into the portfolio in 1997, and it has stood the test of time, regularly receiving awards for the quality and rounded flavour the whisky offers. Rich peat, sweetness and a touch of spice.

HIGHLAND PARK
30 year old
2023 Release

Single malt

PRICE ●●●●●

ABV 45.1%

NOSE Soft toffee and cocoa nibs initially, then waves of waxy tropical fruit and aromatic spice. Ginger, caraway and fennel all play their part.

TASTE More toffee on the palate and a touch of spice from the initial nose comes through. The classic floral peat of Orkney adds influence, although it is very much a subtle background note.

FINISH The finish is remarkably rounded and the sweetness integrates with spice. The smoke comes together with the warmness.

Comments

Highland Park 30 year old is as much about a sense of place as it is about the liquid in a glass. This whisky, with one tiny sip, immediately reminds me of windswept walks on Orcadian moors and coming in from the cold to sit by the fire.

Lochranza

Lochranza is located on the north end of the island of Arran, by Scotland's west coast. Although distillation started in June 1995 at the current distillery, distillation in the area had been present since at least the 1800s. The visitor centre was opened two years later in 1997 by Queen Elizabeth II, who was presented with two casks for Princes William and Harry. The casks are still resting in Warehouse 1 on the island. Lochranza produces a primarily unpeated spirit bottled under the Arran single malt brand, but also distilled limited batches of peated new make up until the opening of its sister distillery Lagg in 2019, on the south end of Arran. Today, the second distillery is dedicated to peated spirit, while Lochranza focuses on its unpeated style. The peated spirit from Lochranza was bottled under the name Machrie Moor, named after a peat bog on the island. Whisky from Lochranza is bottled with natural colour without any chill-filtration and tends to have a minimum ABV of 46%. In 2019, the distillery rebranded with a pristine new bottle design, and in *Whisky Magazine*'s Icons of Whisky Scotland awards it won the title of Brand Innovator of the Year.

LOCHRANZA
Arran Amarone

Single malt

PRICE ●○○○○

ABV 50%

NOSE Following analysis of the colour of this whisky, the drinker can expect fresh berries and fruit aromas. Delving deeper, there is a note of rose petal and perhaps even some subtle jasmine.

TASTE The fruity character of this whisky is enhanced on the palate, with ripe Rainier cherries adding lots of characteristics. There is oak here too, but it is a background flavour dominated by the fruit.

FINISH This whisky has a long and lasting finish with much more of the spice coming through than on the palate. It is a triumph of how active wine casks can be used to create a truly memorable whisky.

Comments

This whisky is a perfect example of a full-bodied spirit character and powerful cask influence existing in harmony. The spirit at Lochranza is flexible and able to work well in a variety of different cask types.

Tobermory

Tobermory distillery is located in the town of the same name on the island of
Mull, off the west coast of Scotland. John Sinclair, a local kelp trader, set out
to build a distillery in 1797 and applied for a lease of 57 acres of land in an area
known as Ledaig. However, although his application to build housing and a
distillery was initially rejected, John did not give up, and managed to establish
Ledaig distillery one year later at Tobermory. After operating on the island for
over a hundred years, the distillery was forced to shut down in the 1930s when
the Great Depression caused the demand for whisky to plummet. It would
remain closed for four decades before being renovated and reopening in the
early 1970s, but would soon close once again. Somewhere along the way the
distillery also changed its name to Tobermory and, like many Scotch distilleries,
was forced to cease production in the 1980s. Not until 1993 would the distillery
be brought back to life again under the ownership of spirits company Burn
Stewart Distillers, which in turn was acquired by Distell in 2013. By then, the
distillery was in need of renovation and maintenance work, and was shut down
by the new owners to put the changes in place before restarting production
in 2019. Today, Tobermory distillery produces a gin as well as its peated and
unpeated single malts. The unpeated single malt is bottled under the Tobermory
name, while the peated spirit is, appropriately, called Ledaig after the original
distillery name and area where it was founded.

TOBERMORY
Ledaig 18 year old

Single malt

PRICE ●●●○○

ABV   46.3%

NOSE Honey and rhubarb are immediately noticeable on the nose. The smoke is well integrated and leads to beautiful tangerine zest and tropical juice.

TASTE More tropical fruit, this time moving into melon and lemon zest, as well as sea-sprayed peat with salted peanut butter.

FINISH The smoke becomes more pronounced and accompanied by a touch of salted aniseed (anise).

Comments

Ledaig has been produced at Tobermory for some decades now and showcases another excellent location where smoky whisky is made to the finest quality. The smoke influence is still conspicuous yet softer and more integrated than in some other whiskies from the Scottish islands.

TOBERMORY
12 year old

Single malt

PRICE ●○○○○

ABV   46.3%

NOSE   Pear tart with rich all-butter pastry. A spoon of tangy crème fraîche sweetened with icing (confectioners') sugar.

TASTE   Waxy with lots of bruised apple skins and apricot compote. The mouthfeel of this relatively youthful whisky is a brilliant surprise: thick and unctuous.

FINISH   Orange oil, vanilla yoghurt with dates and toffee. The fruit builds and finishes long with those orchard fruit notes.

Comments

When the rebranded Tobermory 12 year old was launched I was thrilled by its mouthfeel. The distillery makes both peated and unpeated whisky, and neither compromises on quality.

TOBERMORY
21 year old

Single malt

PRICE ●●●●○

ABV 46.3%

NOSE A rich and nutty nose of toasted hazelnuts and pine nuts. There is treacle toffee and a touch of warming spice as well.

TASTE Soft and nutty marzipan wrapped around fruit cake laced with fiery ginger. Soft and sweet citrus peels add beautiful freshness to this whisky.

FINISH A drying, leather quality and some bitter orange. There is browned caramel as well as some of the toasted oily nuts found on the nose.

Comments

Tobermory 21 year old has had a great influence from sherry casks. The heavy, waxy spirit character is perfectly suited to maturation in rich, spice-laden casks. It is great to taste coastal whiskies in which smoke is absent, and that focus more on the saline elements of the spirit.

Talisker

The story goes that in 1830 the MacAskill brothers rowed from Eigg to Skye to start up Talisker distillery by Loch Harport on the famous island's west coast. (However, being Highland Clearance-era landlords, we might assume they had the coin to get someone to do the rowing for them.) The distillery's spirit is often associated with its coastal character, which is fitting given its waterside location, and uses medium-peated malt in combination with worm-tub condensers to produce a whisky commonly described as having notes of black pepper, brine and seaweed. The distillery burned down in the 1960s but was rebuilt a couple of years later. Talisker's maltings closed about a decade later and the distillery started receiving its malts from Glen Ord in the Highlands instead. Today, Talisker is an important part of the Diageo single malt portfolio. In 2022, following Diageo's £185 million investment in Scottish tourism, the visitor experience was completely transformed with a new interactive facility and revamped distillery tours. The new visitor experience highlights and demonstrates Talisker's motto: 'Made by the sea'. The whisky is recognised as one of the Six Classic Malts of Scotland, the keystone of Diageo's malts portfolio, alongside Cragganmore, Lagavulin, Glenkinchie, Dalwhinnie and Oban.

TALISKER
18 year old

Single malt

PRICE ●●●●○

ABV 45.8%

NOSE Fresh and fruity plums and orange peel are both present on initial nosing, then the aromas develop into butterscotch and elegant peat billowing from a distant cottage.

TASTE Immediately very warming and brimful of chilli spice, white pepper and fresh orange. Then more smoke and another waft of the cottage fireplace. This whisky has lovely notes of orange oil.

FINISH Long, full-bodied and packed with that beautiful chilli spice. Think fresh ginger crushed with dried chilli (red pepper) flakes.

Comments

Many years ago, as my journey through whisky was just beginning, I remember this being one of the first premium whiskies I treated myself to. I bought a glass in a bar and savoured it for what felt like a whole evening, amazed at how much complexity there was within such a humble liquid. It was in that moment that my passion was ignited and I realised I wanted to expand my knowledge on the subject.

TALISKER
25 year old

Single malt

PRICE ●●●●●

ABV 45.8%

NOSE Polished wood and aniseed (anise) appear immediately on the nose; there is also a fruit element in the form of ripe bananas, tart apples and tangerine.

TASTE On the palate, notes of heather honey and rich caramel sprinkled with flaked sea salt materialise initially, before more fruit, this time in the form of juicy peaches.

FINISH The smoke is so well integrated it becomes sweet and delicate, not a dominating note at all. Fragrant oak and a touch of cracked black pepper.

Comments

I was fortunate enough to try this early on in my Scotch whisky journey, sampling it on Skye, overlooking Loch Harport, which seemed otherworldly at the time. There was a rainbow dancing over the waves and the air was filled with seaweed. Drinking this very special whisky in such exceptional surroundings put everything into laser focus, heightening the flavours.

Ardbeg

Ardbeg distillery is located on the southern coast of Islay and dates back to 1815, when founder John Macdougall took out his distillery licence. Over the following decades, a community sprang up around the distillery. The whisky was made using heavily peated malt from its own floor maltings until the mid 1970s, after which supply switched to the Port Ellen maltings, Ardbeg is known – and loved – for its sweet and smoky style. However, its popularity has not always secured it prosperity, and the distillery has been through a rocky path to reach the cult status it has today, closing down and changing owner several times. The most significant change for the distillery came in 1997, when the Glenmorangie Company bought Ardbeg and reopened it the following year. Over the subsequent decade, Ardbeg released incremental iterations of its maturing spirit, all distilled in 1998: Very Young (6 year old), Still Young (8 year old), Almost There (9 year old) and Renaissance (10 year old). This 'peaty path to maturity' culminated with the launch of the flagship Ardbeg 10 year old. Around this time, the distillery also launched the Ardbeg Committee with the focus of ensuring that the distillery never had to close again, thereby securing jobs for the small island. Since its reopening in the late 1990s, Ardbeg has managed to gain popularity around the world with its heavily peated whisky and innovative spirit. Case in point: in 2011 the distillery even sent some of its whisky to space for a maturation experiment to see how gravity affects the maturing process of the spirit.

ARDBEG
10 year old

Single malt

PRICE ●○○○○

ABV 46%

NOSE Key lime pie and camphor oil mingle to produce a complex whisky. Vanilla ice cream and salty sea spray elevate this coastal expression.

TASTE Medicinal smoke counterbalancing vanilla and lime pickle. There is smoky bacon and salted butter.

FINISH Sweet and lingering with bonfire embers after a beach barbecue. This whisky displays both wood smoke and medicinal saltiness.

Comments

I find Ardbeg 10 year old to be a perfect example of the south coast of Islay. This whisky tastes of the tar road leading to the distillery; it is still sharp and citrusy, however, and balances the peat effectively with freshness.

ARDBEG
25 year old

Single malt

PRICE ● ● ● ● ●

ABV 46%

NOSE On initial nosing there are bursts of smoked cream, menthol oiliness and waxy aniseed (anise). There is a whisky fudge note that helps soften the initial peat.

TASTE Hot and spicy, with beautiful notes of jalapeño and habanero, leading to classic Ardbeg citrus of lime and almost verging on pink grapefruit. The palate finishes sweet and creamy.

FINISH Long and lingering, with lots of sweet smoke, unsurprisingly. Creamy vanilla and a hint of delicate, lightly smoked paprika.

Comments

As Ardbeg matures, there is less influence from the smoke, but no less impact in flavour. This gives the fruity or creamy flavours more chance to showcase themselves, and as a result this 25 year old is a perfectly balanced example of Islay whisky.

Bowmore

Bowmore was the first licensed distillery on Islay (a licence was granted in 1816), but distilling at the site on the shores of Lochindaal has supposedly gone on there since 1779. Today, it produces a medium-peated whisky using some peated barley produced in its own floor maltings. The distillery can also claim the first visit by Queen Elizabeth II to any Scotch whisky distillery. She visited in 1980 and was presented with her own cask. When the whisky was later bottled, it was sold to raise money for local charities. Like many distilleries, Bowmore ceased production during the Second World War in the 1940s and the distillery was commandeered by RAF Coastal Command to assist with the war effort. Acquired by family-owned whisky broker Stanley P. Morrison in 1963, it was launched as a single malt in its own right and became an integral part of the Morrison Bowmore group, which was in turn acquired by Suntory in 1994. Just a year before, Bowmore released the first in its series of Black Bowmore bottlings, heavily sherried single malts that have since garnered legendary status. The distillery has been part of the portfolio of Japanese spirits company Beam Suntory since 2014. The long legacy of Bowmore has positioned it well for luxury partnerships, such as the one unveiled in 2020 with the British car manufacturer Aston Martin, leading to 25 bottles of Black Bowmore DB5 1964 being bottled and priced at £50,000.

BOWMORE
15 year old

Single malt

PRICE ●●○○○

ABV 43%

NOSE Dark chocolate, creamy coffee and sweet raisins. Faint bonfire smoke in the background and some beautiful rich spice.

TASTE Linseed oil and golden syrup mingle with notes of toffee apple and creamy malt. The smoke is light and well integrated.

FINISH Long and rich, with notes of sherry in the form of walnuts and raisins and some lovely fresh kiwi.

Comments

Bowmore represents a style of smoky whisky rarely seen today. It is full of tropical fruit and the iodine or medicinal character is very much a background inclusion, with significantly more wood smoke than the disinfectant note that some peated whiskies can offer.

BOWMORE
18 year old

Single malt

PRICE ●●●●○

ABV 43%

NOSE Creamy salted caramel and soft, ripened fruit with mango, pineapples and juicy guava.

TASTE The exotic fruits continue with a touch of passion fruit and some yellow peach. Grilled peach offers some caramelised notes.

FINISH Long and spiced, with some beautiful notes of tart apple. Some soft creamy coffee and a delicate yet fruity smoke, as if banana wood has been set alight.

Comments

This 18-year-old Bowmore has been matured predominantly in American oak casks. I find that as this happens, the smoke becomes far less pronounced and the fruit-driven characteristics of the distillate are allowed to showcase themselves. A tropical note is particularly apparent in older Bowmore expressions.

BOWMORE
25 year old Rare Find
Gleann Mòr

Single malt

PRICE ●●●●●

ABV 53.1%

NOSE Charred pineapple with some chilli spice and dying embers of a barbecue fire. Chocolate and cinnamon add depth.

TASTE The richness is found on the palate with chilli chocolate and stem (preserved) ginger. There is a touch of ripe mango.

FINISH The smoke is more pronounced than expected given the palate, turning damp and earthy. A note of espresso lingers after the fruit dissipates.

Comments

Having spent a significant portion of the maturation in flavourful sherry casks, this particular Bowmore has taken on more richness and density than I would normally expect. The richness has not, however, masked the beautiful elegance and fresh fruit salad usually present. This example shows how the right casks can enhance a fantastically unique spirit while taking it in a different direction.

Bruichladdich

Bruichladdich (pronounced 'brook-*lad*die') was built near Port Charlotte on Islay in 1881. In its early days the spirit from the distillery would have been used for blends, and went through multiple owners before being shut down in 1994. The Victorian distillery was resurrected in 2001 and has worked progressively towards an increasingly dynamic and sustainable future for the industry. From 2020 onwards, the distillery has sourced 100 percent of its electricity from renewable sources, making it one of the first distilleries to be B Corp Certified. Bruichladdich was also the first distillery on Islay to grow and use barley from the island for its whisky. Today, more than 50 per cent of the distillery's barley requirements can be harvested on Islay. It produces three types of spirit: unpeated spirit under the Bruichladdich name, peated spirit called Port Charlotte after the nearby village and finally Octomore, which takes heavily peated whisky to the next level with its ppm levels of over 100. All the single malt expressions here are bottled on the island, following the transformation of an old warehouse into a bottling hall.

BRUICHLADDICH
Black Art 11.1

Single malt

PRICE ●●●●●

ABV 44.2%

NOSE Freshly harvested seaweed covered in white pepper and fragrant clove. There is also toffee and salted caramel, signalling a sweet and rich whisky.

TASTE A hint of lemon and pine nuts topped with sea salt. More caramel and some dark cherries and milk chocolate.

FINISH Briny without being smoky; earthy and zingy with some fresh grapefruit.

Comments

The Bruichladdich distillery has gained a reputation for being exceptionally transparent with the cask make-up of their whiskies. That is until Black Art started being released annually. This expression is the result of careful blending and cask selection, and ensures that some mystery still surrounds Bruichladdich.

BRUICHLADDICH
Octomore 14.3

Single malt

PRICE ●●●●○

ABV 61.4%

NOSE Sweet cereal mixed with honeyed malt, the peat smoke is prominent here and offers notes of smoked meat with stone fruits.

TASTE Very structured oak notes and some coconut and toffee. There are also some floral notes of honeysuckle and red berries.

FINISH Spicy and long, with the peat playing the main role. Salted caramel and sea spray make this a great expression of an Islay icon.

Comments

Drinking an Octomore is as much an experience as it is a simple glass of whisky. When this was first created, the peat rating printed on the bottle was almost a warning and worn as a badge of honour. However, over the 14 sets of releases the spirit has become exceptional and well matured to offer more than just shock factor.

Bunnahabhain

On the shores of the Sound of Islay, on a strip of land on Islay's north coast facing Jura, sits the Victorian distillery of Bunnahabhain (pronounced 'boo-na-*hah*-ven'), first founded in 1881. The pier, which can still be found at the distillery today, was integral to the distillery, as it relied heavily on sea trade due to its remote location. The distillery remained fairly isolated from the rest of the island until the introduction of a new road in the 1960s. The road meant that Bunnahabhain became more accessible by land, so it could be reached by supplies and transport its spirit by vehicle. A second pair of stills was installed in 1963 to increase production, and over a decade later the Bunnahabhain 12 year old was launched to the world. Historically, the distillery produced both peated and unpeated spirit to supply blenders throughout various eras of its existence. Today, the distillery is unusual on Islay for predominantly producing unpeated spirit, although both styles are still made. Bunnahabhain is notable for the fact that all of its whisky is bottled with only its natural colour and without the use of chill-filtration. The peated spirit is predominantly bottled under the name Moine, which means 'smoky' in Scottish Gaelic.

BUNNAHABHAIN
18 year old

Single malt

PRICE ●●●●○

ABV 46.3%

NOSE An initial dense nose of rich walnut loaf topped with coffee crème. There is also a touch of nutmeg, making the nose intriguing.

TASTE The density of the nose continues, with fruit and nut chocolate becoming apparent. Roasted chestnuts and fresh leather also assert themselves.

FINISH The finish is long and spiced – cinnamon and Scottish tablet assist with this. There is also sea spray adding a touch of salt.

Comments

Bunnahabhain is almost as remote as it is possible for a distillery to be, but once there you are treated to some incredible panoramic views and stunning scenery. This whisky is testament to this remoteness, with old-style sherry casks, which would have been imported by sea, housing rich and full-bodied spirit creating whisky that will warm you up on even the coldest of days.

BUNNAHABHAIN
40 year old

Single malt

PRICE ● ● ● ● ●

ABV 41.9%

NOSE Damp and sweet oak are first noted, leading to sweet, ripe tropical fruit and some soft blanched almonds.

TASTE The palate offers more tropical fruit as this whisky asserts itself with guava and some dragon fruit before softer, more recognisable pineapple cubes emerge.

FINISH Long, and becoming sweeter over time. Vanilla from the oak perfectly complements the fruit salad offered by the nose.

Comments

The pinnacle of Bunnahabhain's aged expressions, this 40-year-old has, uncommonly for the distillery, spent its entire maturation in American oak. I adore this whisky and I am reminded of the magic of Islay every time I taste it. It is a welcoming whisky, straightforward with great conversation, much like the local workforce who call the island home.

BUNNAHABHAIN
Fèis Île 2023 1998 Manzanilla Cask Finish

Single malt

PRICE ● ● ● ● ●

ABV 52.3%

NOSE A nose of dairy fudge straight from the pan. There is also some dried apricot providing fruity character, along with a touch of freshly sliced green apple.

TASTE On the palate the salt of the manzanilla sherry cask starts to show, with rich nutty notes of walnut and macadamia.

FINISH The finish is spicy and drying, with the stone fruits really making their presence felt.

Comments

This 2023 Islay Malts Festival (or Fèis Île) expression is an excellent example of what Bunnahabhain release annually for the festival. Exposed to a long finish of six years before being bottled at cask strength, we see Bunnahabhain take on a rich and fruity flavour with use of manzanilla sherry casks not often seen in the Scotch industry.

Kilchoman

Kilchoman (pronounced 'kil-*ho*-man') is one of the more recent additions to the Islay whisky scene, having been founded in 2005 by Anthony Wills at Rockside Farm, making it the first new distillery to be built on the island in over 124 years. The small-scale distillery started out by producing only a few hundred thousand litres per year using traditional methods including floor maltings, two sets of copper pot stills and dunnage warehouses, but has since more than doubled its production while staying true to its 100 per cent Islay philosophy. Kilchoman also built a bottling hall, ensuring the entire process from grain to bottle can all be done on the farm. As a nod to tradition, but also an acknowledgment of the land's influence on whisky's character, Kilchoman uses locally grown barley for approximately 20 per cent of its production. The purest expression of this barley is the 100 per cent Islay series, which uses only barley from Rockside Farm that is malted, mashed, fermented, distilled, matured and bottled on site. The distillery is currently producing 640,000 litres (169,000 US gallons) of pure alcohol each year and uses a long fermentation of 85 hours to achieve floral sweetness and citrus notes. Kilchoman also makes a peated spirit, using peat sourced from Islay.

KILCHOMAN
Machir Bay

Single malt

PRICE ●○○○○

ABV 46%

NOSE Underneath the earthy smoke there are layers of dry hay, freshly baked shortbread and candied lime peel.

TASTE Lemon and lime curd with some guava, more soft vanilla and a touch of raisin. The smoke is subtle but well integrated into the fruity tones.

FINISH A herbal edge starts to become present, with some parsley and a touch of cracked black pepper over butter.

Comments

Kilchoman paved the way for how new distilleries should approach whisky making: a considered approach pairing spirit style with cask type and releasing great whisky at a young age. This has continued, and we are fortunate to get some truly fantastic whiskies from the western Islay farm distillery.

KILCHOMAN
Comraich Batch 6

Single malt

PRICE ●●●●●

ABV 53.8%

NOSE Notes of baked apples and hay are present on the nose. Vanilla and soft spice are also detectable.

TASTE Fresh fruits and some mandarin zest are apparent on the palate. This is a lively whisky with some white pepper and the classic herbal smoke of Kilchoman.

FINISH Long and lively, with some more citrus zest and even a touch of apricot eau de vie and white chocolate.

Comments

The Comraich releases have only ever been sold in selected whisky bars across the world that have been chosen by Kilchoman as suitable homes for these bottles. It has been a fascinating series and I truly believe that Batch 6 is the best yet. There is so much intrigue, and the finishing Calvados casks work so well with the herbal smoke of the distillery's new make spirit.

Glenkinchie

Glenkinchie is the Lowland home of Johnnie Walker and was founded 15 miles outside of Edinburgh in 1825 by two farmers. Until 1837 it was known as the Milton distillery, hinting at the site's origins, until it changed its name after a rebuild in reference to the clear Kinchie Burn that still runs past the distillery today. The surrounding area is referred to as 'the garden of Scotland' due to its fertile land, and the distillery itself was long known colloquially as the Edinburgh malt, as it was the closest whisky distillery to the capital until the return of whisky making in the city itself in 2019, at Old Chain Pier. The distillery produces a slightly sulphury style of new make spirit using two large stills and worm-tub condensers, but this characteristic matures out and leaves a beautiful floral, moderately fruity character. Glenkinchie is one of Diageo's Four Corners of Scotland alongside Cardhu, Caol Ila and Clynelish. In 2020 the new visitor experience opened, providing an immersive tour set in the distillery's traditional Victorian red brick warehouses.

GLENKINCHIE
Distillers Edition

Single malt

PRICE ●●○○○

ABV 43%

NOSE Barley sugar and damp hay fill the nose with a beautiful elegance traditionally associated with Lowland whiskies.

TASTE The softness continues with lemon balm along with dry cereal and malt influence before the creamier and nutty qualities of the finishing cask start to present themselves.

FINISH Nutty and dry with dry-roasted almonds and walnuts. Then come some very delicate citrus peels.

Comments

This classic malt, elevated by time in amontillado sherry casks, is a perfect example of a drier style of whisky with delicious floral notes.

Daftmill

Daftmill is a family farm located in Fife in the Scottish Lowlands. From growing produce such as barley, the farm took the step of applying for planning permission to convert their old mill buildings into a distillery in 2003. The stills and the mash tuns were made by the coppersmiths Forsyths in Speyside, but all the other equipment and manual work were sourced from craftsmen local to the area. By St Andrew's Day in 2005, the distillery had received its licence and was ready to get production under way. It uses the barley from the farm to make its whisky and operates seasonally to coexist with the farm. This results in production taking place primarily during the winter months, when the farming business is less busy, but it falls silent when sowing begins in spring. Operating on this basis was once very common across Scottish distilleries, when the distillers also had to tend to their farms. Today, the distillery has become a cult sensation on account of its farm-to-bottle ethos and quality spirit, while its team's quiet confidence and media shyness has endeared the distillery to whisky enthusiasts.

DAFTMILL
2010 Summer Release

Single malt

PRICE ●●●●○

ABV 46%

NOSE Initially very citrusy with lemon and grapefruit, then developing into mineral sweetness with marzipan and wet barley.

TASTE Lemon zest, honey and a touch of vanilla. There are some spicy characteristics as well, with light chilli and oak tannin.

FINISH This whisky finishes mid-palate with the same sweetness and almond character expected from the nose. Finally, some faint turmeric or gorse flower emerges.

Comments

Daftmill's first release was one of the most hotly anticipated from the contemporary wave of distilleries. This was in part due to the length of time the whisky was allowed to mature. Because of the farm, the whisky was allowed to mellow for far longer than the compulsory three years, and this in turn has built a strong fan base for this Fife distillery.

Ailsa Bay

Ailsa Bay was built adjacent to the Girvan grain distillery in South Ayrshire, and opened in 2009. Designed with versatility in mind, Ailsa Bay produces a variety of spirit styles, which are predominantly used for the blends of owner William Grant & Sons. It produces both unpeated and peated whisky, and the latter is also bottled as a single malt release. The whisky undergoes what the distiller calls 'micromaturation', where the new make spirit is first matured in casks that have previously held Hudson Baby Bourbon, before a secondary maturation in virgin, first-fill or refill American oak. The distillery is notable for having stainless-steel condensers on some of its stills, intended for production of more sulphury spirit, while others retain the more common copper type. The first releases of single malt featured a bespoke cork decorated with granite, a nod to the island Ailsa Craig, located off the coast from Girvan, which is home to an old granite quarry popular for the production of curling stones.

AILSA BAY
1.2 Sweet Smoke

Single malt

PRICE ●●○○○

ABV 48.9%

NOSE The nose opens with damp campfire embers after a bonfire on a beach, then soft stone fruits and custard creams add to the complex nose.

TASTE Vanilla and sweet notes of honesty and orange complement the smoke, which has now become fragrant and earthy.

FINISH There is spice derived from the use of virgin oak, and some orchard fruits start to appear.

Comments

When Ailsa Bay was first launched as a single malt and I started learning about the distillery set-up, I was fascinated by the scientific detail that goes into creating the spirit. Most of Ailsa Bay's production is reserved for blending, but a small amount of peated spirit is created and bottled as release 1.2.

Glen Scotia

Glen Scotia is one of three historic distilleries that remain in the Campbeltown region, which was once home to more than 30 distilleries. Although Campbeltown is the smallest whisky region in Scotland, located on the remote Kintyre peninsula, it was known as the whisky capital of the world in its heyday. Glen Scotia produces both peated and unpeated spirit, and has been in production since 1832. Much of its original design has been preserved, such as the still room, fermenters and dunnage warehouse. Since 1999, Glen Scotia has been a part of the Loch Lomond Distillers, later Loch Lomond Group, portfolio. Both the distillery and the Campbeltown region are undergoing something of a renaissance, with the region growing increasingly popular for both whisky drinkers and those looking to start new whisky distilleries, due to its high-quality single malts and historic heritage. Glen Scotia is a key part of the annual Campbeltown Whisky Festival held in May.

GLEN SCOTIA
11 year old
Festival Edition 2023
White Port Finish

Single malt

PRICE ●●○○○

ABV 54.7%

NOSE A fresh start showcasing some notes of spearmint and applewood smoke, then some sweeter fruits develop, such as honeydew melon and canned lychees.

TASTE The palate is interesting, with strong flavours of allspice and vanilla mixed with less common notes of oaked Chardonnay and cream.

FINISH The smoke turns sweet, almost cigar-like, and there are notes of violet and apricot. The white port has done wonders to lengthen the finish here.

Comments

Every year Glen Scotia do a fantastic job with their Campbeltown Malts Festival bottling, this time marrying ashy but light peat with the fruity and rich style of white port.

GLEN SCOTIA
18 year old

Single malt

PRICE ●●●●○

ABV 46%

NOSE A tang from the salty aromas in this whisky can immediately be noticed. There are violets and thick vanilla and toffee notes.

TASTE The creamy, sweet vanilla continues and is joined by notes of pineapple and mandarin before some more of that maritime spice develops.

FINISH The finish is dry and full of lingering spice in the form of cloves and a touch of nutmeg, then some spent vanilla pod (bean) adds subtlety.

Comments

Glen Scotia produces some excellent examples of coastal-style whiskies without necessarily being peated. This 18-year-old is one such example, with the salty and oily characteristics of a long walk on a Kintyre beach.

Glengyle

Glengyle is the distillery nowadays known for producing Kilkerran single malt. It is located in Campbeltown and is one of only three historic distilleries in the area. During the second half of the 1800s, brothers John and William Mitchell ran Springbank distillery, which had been founded by their father, but after a family disagreement William left the family business to set up Glengyle distillery on his own. It was founded in 1872, but suffered like many others during the start of the 20th century, which resulted in Glengyle closing and selling all their stock. The distillery buildings remained and were fairly well preserved thanks to relatively continuous use up until modern times. Several attempts were made to reopen the distillery and then, in November of 2000, the buildings were bought by a new company by the name of Mitchell's Glengyle Ltd, which was headed by Hedley G Wright, the late chairman of J & A Mitchell and Co Ltd, which owns Springbank distillery. The distillery was renovated and production resumed a couple of years later following restoration work. The inaugural release came in 2007 and was branded as Kilkerran to avoid confusion with a blend already using the Glengyle name, and it is now firmly part of the Campbeltown whisky landscape.

GLENGYLE
Kilkerran 12 year old

Single malt

PRICE ●○○○○

ABV 46%

NOSE Cherry bakewell with pastry, sweet royal icing and dried orange. There are notes of toasted marshmallow and milk chocolate.

TASTE Butterscotch and toffee dominate the palate, with sweet lemon peel adding a fresh element.

FINISH Burnt lemon served with New York cheesecake. The finish is long and sweet, and there is the classic weight of Campbeltown whiskies along with the fresh citrus character.

Comments

When Glengyle reopened in 2004 there was much anticipation to see how the whisky would taste. The distillery was built hastily and through salvaging parts from other distilleries, so the spirit character was somewhat unknown when the stills were first fired up. Fortunately, after around two decades worth of whisky making at Glengyle, we see this lost treasure of Scotch whisky reawakened.

GLENGYLE
Kilkerran 16 year old

Single malt

PRICE ●●●○○

ABV 46%

NOSE Lemon and ginger tea are initially present, with some tropical fruit and soft, light caramel. Then emerges a savoury element – honey roast ham, perhaps?

TASTE The oily character of Glengyle comes with lemon balm and light smoke, then fresh raspberry and ginger snap biscuits emerge.

FINISH A nutty character appears in the form of pistachio, and creamy elements develop. Think pistachio ice cream in a waffle cone.

Comments

This is the fourth release of Kilkerran 16 year old, and with the malt predominantly matured in ex-sherry casks, unlike previous years, it is clear that this is by far the richest of the four. Spiced and almost meaty in its presentation, this is an excellent example of what Glengyle can produce.

Springbank

Springbank distillery was founded in 1828 by Archibald Mitchell, becoming Campbeltown's 14th licensed distillery in the process, on the same site as a previous illicit still. The distillery was passed on to Mitchell's sons John and William in 1837, but William eventually left the family business to start his own Campbeltown distillery, Glengyle. John brought his own son into the company and formed the company J & A Mitchell with ownership of Springbank distillery, which has been run by generations of the Mitchell family ever since. It is one of the oldest family-owned distilleries in Scotland. The hardships for Campbeltown distilleries in the first half of the 20th century saw many of them start to shut down, and by 1934, after the closure of the neighbouring distillery Rieclachan, only Springbank and Glen Scotia were left. At the end of the 20th century, during another downturn in Scotch whisky, Springbank continued to sell whisky, but production was infrequent. Though its core style is lightly peated, Springbank has been producing heavily peated spirit under the name Longrow since 1973 and, not satisfied with only producing two spirit styles, a third was added in 1997. This spirit is called Hazelburn and is produced through triple distillation. Today, all three styles are in production at the distillery. The double-distilled, lightly peated Springbank whisky is arguably the most sought-after single malt produced in Scotland, and has ascended to a near-mythical status on account of its family owner's commendable commitment to historic production practices, which create a weighty, delicately smoky, slightly sulphurous spirit like no other.

SPRINGBANK
10 year old

Single malt

PRICE ●○○○○

ABV 46%

NOSE There is a terrific maltiness to this whisky; over time, the fruit starts to develop with notes of rhubarb, green apples and white grapes.

TASTE The fruit carries through with notes of orange zest and mango, then the cereal begins to dominate with oat biscuits and toasted malt.

FINISH The smoke becomes more apparent on the finish with honeycomb toffee and smoked cheese.

Comments

The unmistakable characteristics of Campbeltown whisky are ever present in this classic: oily and coastal with a faint hint of mellow peat smoke and brine. There seems to be some fantastic batch variation in the 10-year-old, but one thing that does not vary is the quality. This is a top-quality whisky, and always well received.

SPRINGBANK
21 year old

Single malt

PRICE ●●●●○

ABV 46%

NOSE A very intriguing nose of tropical fruits such as pineapple and guava mingle with more savoury notes of smoked bacon and the herbal edge of a well-maintained greenhouse.

TASTE The tropical fruit continues, adding mango and coconut to the profile, with deeper notes of cola cubes and old earthen-floor warehouses.

FINISH The finish is long and spicy with charred pineapple, orange zest and toffee, while a note of sour cherries plays in the background.

Comments

Every year there is a new release of aged malt from the warehouses of Campbeltown, usually with very little information about how each has been matured. This is a positive, however, as it allows the drinker to formulate their own opinions of these whiskies without any perceptions about what notes they should find.

SPRINGBANK
Longrow Peated

Single malt

PRICE ●○○○○

ABV 46%

NOSE Creamy vanilla custard presents first, a distinctive note of tangy rhubarb and apple lying underneath. Subtle smoke plays a background note on the nose.

TASTE Balanced, rich and oily, but well integrated with the sweetness perceived on the nose. The soft smoke is a beautiful addition to this full-bodied whisky.

FINISH There are waves of briny smoke and soft vanilla, while the fruit works tirelessly to be assertive.

Comments

First distilled in 1973, Longrow was named after one of the lost distilleries of Campbeltown. It was initially produced to allow Springbank to offer a heavily peated and robust component to blenders, and as proof that an Islay-style malt could be produced on the mainland, but the smoky, double-distilled spirit has been a staple since the 1990s. Today, the Longrow flagship is a No Age Statement release, complemented by a series of annual small-batch releases. Longrow Peated is pleasant and very well balanced. The increase of peat is noticeable from the classic Springbank profile, but it still feels part of the family.

SPRINGBANK
Hazelburn 10 year old

Single malt

PRICE ●●●○○

ABV 46%

NOSE The nose opens very fruity, with pear drops, vanilla-poached apples and some beautiful notes of elderflower and lemon zest.

TASTE Rich and waxy, like biting into a freshly picked Granny Smith apple. More vanilla and some creamy milk chocolate.

FINISH The oily texture of this whisky really does allow for a long and lingering finish, with some fantastic floral notes of violet and sweet cicely.

Comments

Hazelburn is triple distilled and, like Longrow, its name comes from a lost Campbeltown distillery. Springbank has been producing Hazelburn since 1997 and the spirit is described as creamy, delicate and light. If Longrow is the proof that Islay-style malt can be made on the mainland, then Hazelburn is proof that Irish-style malt can be made in Scotland. The triple distillation means much of the flavour comes from the casks that have nurtured the whisky. For this release, only American oak ex-bourbon casks are used, allowing the spirit to brim with luscious orchard notes.

Compass Box

Compass Box was founded in 2000 by John Glaser, who wanted to explore beyond the traditional realms of whisky creation and bottling. Compass Box is a blending house that focuses on innovation, based on the traditional art of blending that built the industry we have today. Experiments from the company include casks of various toasting levels and with bespoke cask designs. Like many companies with humble beginnings, it was originally run from John's kitchen, but quickly grew and the team now operates across two blending rooms in London, with its own maturing stock of casks in Scotland. The first whisky created by Compass Box was the blended grain Hedonism, which remains the flagship product of the blended grain Scotch whisky category to this day. Blended grain whiskies are not often widely available as independent products, but the bottling has become a highly appreciated signature whisky for the company. Whiskies from Compass Box are bottled with natural colour without chill-filtration, and the ethos of the company is also to avoid age statements, as Glaser believes focus should be on character and flavour rather than age. Although Compass Box has core releases that are bottled every year, it has also produced a wide selection of limited releases. For each blend, they detail online which whiskies have been used to create it, along with the quantity of each component and their cask type.

COMPASS BOX
Hedonism

Blended grain

PRICE ●●○○○

ABV 43%

NOSE Delicate coconut and creamy milk chocolate remind me of tiny sweets from a sharing box at Christmas; enticing.

TASTE The palate is brimming with desiccated coconut, ripe banana over caramel waffle with chocolate sauce and just a touch of lemon oil.

FINISH The finish is quite short but not unpleasant, with beautiful continuity of the palate; coconut, chocolate and the addition of orange. This is a very inviting whisky with an exceptionally moreish profile.

Comments

To put out a blended grain whisky as a first release could be seen as a big leap of faith in the product, as the category can often be misunderstood. Compass Box have always believed in their liquid and this is very apparent with this fantastic example. Beautifully soft and sweet, giving consumers a real treat.

COMPASS BOX
Orchard House

Blended malt

PRICE ●○○○○

ABV 46%

NOSE Freshly cut red apple and bright grapefruit give way to apples cooked in pastry and apple sauce.

TASTE Soft cooking apple balances out with zingy lemon and vanilla oak spice. There is a smoky character, almost like the slightly burnt edges of an apple pie.

FINISH The sweetness of this whisky really takes over on the finish with more vanilla and baked apple qualities. Think apples cooked in sugar and spices with a scoop of Cornish ice cream.

Comments

I have always been a fan of how Compass Box put their whiskies together: flavour-led and uncompromising on quality. This expression is no different; it's a versatile whisky as much at home in a highball as it is as a neat whisky.

Cambus

The Cambus distillery was founded in the early 19th century as a malt distillery, after being converted from an old mill. Thirty years later, the founder John Moubray converted the distillery to produce grain whisky instead. Cambus was one of the distilleries to lead the way for grain whisky, which became important for the blended Scotch industry, and was one of the first to implement continuous stills for grain whisky distillation. The distillery used two Stein stills to begin with, but later installed a Coffey still in the middle of the 19th century. Cambus had to shut its doors when a fire destroyed most of the distillery in 1914, but managed to reopen 23 years later, only to be shut down again during the Second World War. When it eventually reopened, the owners invested in the site once again to expand and improve the distillery, which kept it producing whisky until its imminent closure and demolition. The Cambus distillery was located in the Lowlands region of Scotland, in Clackmannanshire, but was demolished in 1993. The whisky that remains is often highly sought after, particularly the older expressions, and stands as a shining example of how distinctive and characterful grain whisky can be when well matured in a quality cask.

CAMBUS
40 year old
Douglas Laing XOP Range

Single grain

PRICE ●●●●●

ABV 41.3%

NOSE Tropical fruits of mango and pineapple play host to fresh coconut cream, vanilla scents and brown sugar before fragrant oak is introduced in the form of sandalwood.

TASTE On the palate there is creamy and strong Arabica coffee and a note of lemon mousse arrives. This is a sweet whisky with lots of toffee and delicate liquorice.

FINISH White chocolate with passion fruit conserve and more coconut cream are present on the finish. It is mid-length and moreish with the sweetness of roasted hazelnuts.

Comments

When grain whisky like this is allowed to mature untouched for several decades, there is something of a magical outcome: every morsel of harshness is removed and left behind is a soft, gentle and incredibly alluring whisky. This is an often-overlooked category of Scotch whisky, but one that is gaining more admirers in whisky-drinking circles.

Gordon & MacPhail

Gordon & MacPhail is a family-owned company based in Elgin, near Inverness, which focuses on premium spirits. Gordon & MacPhail was initially established as a grocery business in 1895 by James Gordon and John Alexander MacPhail. The pair sought to acquire a variety of single malt whiskies to complement the international groceries such as teas, coffees and wine that they had already acquired. A young John Urquhart joined the business as an apprentice under the two founders and later went on to develop an impressive portfolio of maturing casks from Scottish distilleries. To this day, John's descendants are still involved in the company. Gordon & MacPhail is the proud owner of the Benromach and Cairn distilleries, both located in Speyside. Benromach was acquired in 1993 as a result of a long-standing ambition for the Urquhart family to own their own distillery. The Cairn, which sits in the Cairngorms National Park, opened its doors to visitors in 2022. Throughout the years Gordon & MacPhail have maintained and expanded their cask library, which includes casks from now-closed distilleries, rare stock from the mid 1900s and single-cask releases with intriguing finishes.

BENROMACH
1982 Gordon & Macphail
Private Collection

Single malt

PRICE ●●●●●

ABV 59.9%

NOSE Freshly peeled orange, lightly cooked apples and fragrant vanilla initially, which develops into a note of fresh cranberries and raspberries.

TASTE Spice in the form of red chilli, and raspberry and strawberry salad garnished with mint and a touch of tarragon.

FINISH Long and spicy, with more of the chilli notes presenting themselves and growing sweeter over time.

Comments

This whisky sits within Gordon & MacPhail's Private Collection series and spends 19 years in a sherry cask before being transferred to a Burgundy cask for another 20 years. This has been bottled somewhat independently by Benromach's parent company, as it is a seismic deviation from the house style now created at the distillery. This is, however, a fantastic whisky and is well deserving of its place within the Private Collection livery.

TORMORE
G&M 2000

Single malt

PRICE ●●●●○

ABV 58.8%

NOSE Lemon and lime are first apparent with fresh peels tossed in caster (superfine) sugar, then there is some vanilla fudge with rich sweetened cream.

TASTE This whisky is zingy and dances across the palate with notes of pineapple, coconut and key lime pie, before lime- and chilli-flavoured white chocolate is apparent.

FINISH There is a length and spice to this that is rewarding and pleasant as the spice builds before the final introduction of that tart note of green mango.

Comments

The Tormore distillery produces, from a spirit character point of view, one of the most instantly recognisable spirits around. Thick, sweet and nostalgic, it brings back happy memories of sweet shops in the summer. It is therefore no wonder that the team at Elixir Distillers was so keen to take ownership of the distillery and brand. I look forward to seeing what the coming years have in store for the Tormore as it begins to emerge as a real favourite here at SCOTCH.

GLENBURGIE
21 year old
Gordon & MacPhail
Distillery Labels

Single malt

PRICE ●●●●○

ABV 46%

NOSE Stewed orchard fruit, such as red apples and sweet apricots, are initially present. They are then joined by buttery sweetness and a hint of toasted oak in the form of vanilla.

TASTE The buttery sweetness of rich caramel is still present, this time forming a beautiful base to a classic tarte tatin alongside a touch of spice from the oak.

FINISH Long, dry and very inviting with more cooked fruit. These notes are becoming slightly baked, with more oak presenting itself at the end.

Comments

Gordon & MacPhail are custodians of some of Speyside's most elusive whiskies, whether that be from closed distilleries or distilleries operating to provide world-famous blends with key components. It is therefore testament to their stock reserves that whiskies like this can be released on an annual basis.

Berry Bros. & Rudd

Berry Bros. & Rudd started out as a grocery shop at 3 St James's Street in London in 1698. The shop featured exotic wares such as teas and spices, but would come to focus on stronger goods like wines and spirits as time went on. Today it is renowned for being one of the oldest wine and spirit merchants in the UK. The long history and dedication to quality products have earned the merchant two Royal Warrants during its 300-plus years of existence. The company started bottling casks under its own label in the early 19th century, making Berry Bros. & Rudd Britain's oldest independent spirits bottler. London's 3 St James's Street is still home to the shop where customers can purchase both official bottlings as well as the independent bottlings and blends . Berry Bros. & Rudd also sought to develop its own brands, and created Cutty Sark blended Scotch whisky in 1923, which became an exceedingly popular blend in the American market. Cutty Sark was later traded for the Glenrothes single malt brand, which was subsequently sold back to the Edrington Group. Berry Bros. & Rudd's independent bottlings are still going strong and its spirits portfolio has been expanded with the addition of No.3 London Dry Gin and The King's Ginger liqueur.

BERRY BROS. & RUDD
Blended Malt
44 year old

Blended malt

PRICE ●●●●●

ABV 52.6%

NOSE Freshly opened, creamy coconut initially jumps out of the glass. There is soft, runny honey and salted butter on seeded toast.

TASTE The palate is incredibly fruity with lots of exotic fruit such as lychee, yuzu and delicate eucalyptus. There is much complexity here and the mouthfeel is incredibly viscous.

FINISH The thickness of the palate continues and the finish is long, lingering and builds to a zingy, fresh white peach.

Comments

Berry Bros. & Rudd have a history of blending, so it is no surprise that treasures like this have been released from their warehouses. This whisky has sweetness, richness and body in abundance.

Johnnie Walker

Johnnie Walker is a brand of blended Scotch whiskies named after Scottish grocer John Walker, who started his business in Kilmarnock in 1820. He began blending whiskies for consistency instead of selling single malts, which could be inconsistent in character at the time. Following John's passing the family business was taken over by his son Alexander, who continued the blending business and developed the brand, launching Walker's Old Highland Blend in 1857. As the world began to open up through rail travel and ships in the mid 1800s, which transported goods to various continents, Alexander saw an exciting opportunity for his blended whisky to reach more customers. In 1867 Alexander introduced the signature square bottle with the angled label to stand out on the shelves, and in 1908 the popular English illustrator Tom Browne designed the striding man that has decorated bottles ever since. Today, Johnnie Walker blended Scotch is available in over 180 markets and is the bestselling Scotch whisky in the world. There are a variety of expressions that also include premium versions such as the No Age Statement Johnnie Walker Blue Label.

JOHNNIE WALKER
Black Label

Blended Scotch whisky

PRICE ●○○○○

ABV 40%

NOSE Immediately there are notes of caramelised banana and toffee sauce, then some spice comes through with cloves before a faint whiff of wood smoke emerges.

TASTE More banana notes on the palate, with bread and butter pudding adding a welcome creaminess, as well as malt and grain notes of toasted maize with a hint of coal fire smoke.

FINISH The fruit builds and more sherry notes start to unfold, sultanas and almonds in particular.

Comments

An unbelievably versatile whisky that is as much at home in a cocktail or mixed drink as it is over ice or neat. Sales of Johnnie Walker as a brand are estimated at around 138 million bottles per year for 2023, which is absolutely staggering and testament to the unique and innovative brand that has been created.

JOHNNIE WALKER
Blue Label

Blended Scotch whisky

PRICE ●●●●○

ABV 40%

NOSE Mellow and dry with a beautiful, subtle wood smoke on the nose alongside raisins and crème brûlée.

TASTE Layers of soft smoke, candied fruit covered in dark honey and delicate vanilla mirroring the nose.

FINISH Velvety hot chocolate with ginger and a gentle whisper of smoke coming from Scotland's island distilleries.

Comments

Of the 22 million casks maturing in Scotland as we speak, the blenders at Johnnie Walker deem only 1 in 10,000 casks of sufficient quality to be part of Blue Label's final make-up. This demonstrates the care taken to ensure this premium blend maintains its position as one of the most highly regarded and well recognised Scotch whiskies in the world.

Cameron's Afterword

I am fortunate to work with hundreds, if not thousands, of different Scotch whiskies that vary in any given year. The excitement of curating a list of over 500 Scotch whiskies for SCOTCH visitors to enjoy never dwindles. From the oldest and rarest whiskies in the world to some of Scotland's most revered warehouses to the swathe of new distilleries marking their place in Scotland's whisky industry, the most rewarding part of my job is seeing visitors to SCOTCH fall in love with the whisky I have suggested. Sharing that excitement sparks the start of a journey of discovery on two fronts. Firstly, I have the opportunity to find out customers' preferences and where they want the experience to take them. Secondly, upon gaining this insight, I can delve into our vast selection of whisky to guide them on a truly memorable experience.

The landscape of Scotch whisky is evolving, and fascinating times are ahead for the industry. Innovation is at the forefront of the creation of new releases, which are seamlessly uniting the legends, fables and myths of distilleries with considered production practices. This combination creates a complete product, one that answers the 'why' – why it has been created and why it is relevant to the distillery's history – as well as the 'how' – the use of different technical practices to introduce new flavours, whether through cask selection and blending or using different yeast strains to enhance certain flavours in

fermentation. This combination of approaches is holistic and does not focus merely on one side or the other. That, for me, is refreshing, as it is often these tales and legends that are the points of enthusiastic discussion when we introduce guests to new whisky in SCOTCH.

In a world where connectivity is valued so highly, whisky has the ability to connect and disconnect us in perfect harmony. It has the capacity, through one sip, to transport us to any number of remote locations across Scotland, even to a particular distillery. It also allows us to disconnect from the fast-paced world and savour the time, care and attention to detail that the distillery workers, blenders and malt masters have put into creating the finished product. This is one of the main reasons I fell in love with the subject. We are also seeing an increase in technology used to enjoy Scotch in the modern world, and this is something to be praised too. With online tasting sessions connecting lovers of whisky from all over the world, to apps that can be used to keep a digital record of personal collections or to discover more about historical bottlings, technology is at the heart of the next generation of Scotch whisky drinkers' experience.

I look forward to continuing to grow our offering here at SCOTCH and welcoming as many new visitors and returning enthusiasts as possible.

Index

Acknowledgements

Cameron

It is of the utmost importance to acknowledge that the journey of creating and completing a project such as this would not have been possible without the help, support and patience of my family, close friends and work colleagues. They have ensured I stayed true and honest to the task at hand, and that the work I have created is representative of my ethos and experience in my current position.

Both the whisky and hospitality industries are filled with incredible talent and within Edinburgh there is a really wonderful feeling of community. These industries are two hubs which nurture talent and ensure a lasting reputation for top class professionals in both fields is maintained. I began my journey in SCOTCH almost ten years ago and was instantly in awe of the passion and enthusiasm of my former colleague and unknowing mentor, Fraser Robson. He remains a dear friend, and it was his generosity with his time and knowledge that encouraged me to pursue a career in the whisky industry.

The support and enthusiasm shown to me by the hotel's former General Manager, Mr Richard Cooke, was inspiring. His trust in our operation and love for SCOTCH continues to motivate us every day to ensure our whisky bar is always performing to the highest standards. I would also like to express my sincerest gratitude to my team here at The Balmoral for supporting me to put my passion into print. Within our grand hotel, which has dominated Edinburgh's skyline since 1902, we have delivered some of the highest standards of hospitality and I am forever grateful to be a part of this story.

Lastly and most importantly, I would like to give a huge thank you to my family, particularly my parents who have always encouraged me to be curious and to embrace opportunities given to me, and to my partner Lauren, for supporting me in continuing to do what I truly love – sharing my passion and enthusiasm for whisky, Scotland and Scottish hospitality with my guests. These three things give me purpose at work every day and ensure I have the drive to make our offering better today than it was yesterday. Without her encouragement and grounded realism, this would be a much less clear task.

Moa

It has been a pleasure to work with The Balmoral to write this book, which I hope will be a helpful and enjoyable guide to Scotch whisky for anyone who might pick it up.

I never expected to find myself involved in the drinks industry but I am so happy that my path led me here as it is such a fantastic world to be a part of.

It would not have been possible for me to be a part of this project without the wonderful support of my husband, friends and family, so I am immensely grateful to them. I want to include a special thank you to my supportive parents who always let me run as fast as I could in any direction I pleased, even when it was difficult to keep up.

Picture Credits

The publishers would like to acknowledge and thank all the whisky distilleries, brands and their agents who have kindly provided images for this book.

Adelphi: Ardnamurchan; Angus Dundee Distillers: Glencadam, Tomintoul; Bacardi/John Dewar & Sons: Aberfeldy, Craigellachie, Royal Brackla; Beam Suntory: Bowmore, Glen Garioch; Brown-Forman: Benriach (photo John Paul 112), The GlenDronach (photo Peter Sandground 86); Campari Group: Glen Grant; Compass Box; Diageo: Cambus Cooperage, Clynelish (photo Till Britze 72), Dailuaine, Dalwhinnie (photo Jakub Iwanicki 74), Glenkinchie (photo Simon Hird 184), Johnnie Walker (photo Simon Hird 212, Andy Bate 215), Talisker; Distell Group: Bunnahabhain, Deanston, Tobermory (photo Jakub Iwanicki 160); Edrington: Highland Park, The Glenrothes, The Macallan; GlenAllachie (photo Andy Bate 124); Gordon & McPhail: Benromach; Tormore G&M 2000 (208), Glenburgie (209); Ian Macleod Distillers: Tamdhu; International Beverages: Balblair; Isle of Arran Distillers: Lochranza; J&G Grant: Glenfarclas (30, photo John Paul 126); Kilchoman (photo Konrad Borkowski 181); La Martiniquaise: Glen Moray; Lalique Group: The Glenturret; Loch Lomond Group: Glen Scotia; LVMH: Ardbeg, Glenmorangie; Mitchells Glengyle: Glengyle, Springbank (photo @frombarreltobottle 195, 196); Pernord-Ricard: Aberlour, Longmorn, The Glenlivet; Rémy Cointreau: Bruichladdich; Takara Shuzo: Tomatin; Whyte & Mackay: Fettercairn (photo James Wright 80); William Grant & Sons: Ailsa Bay, The Balvenie, Glenfiddich (photo John Paul 129).

Thanks also to Berry Bros & Rudd (187, 210, 211); Decadent Drinks (92) and Douglas Laing & Co (205)Hi

Special photography by Perry Graham for Octopus Publishing Group

Additional photography:
Alamy Stock Photo: Tim Gainey 122, Kim Gordon Bates 155, Iain Masterton 174, SO Photography 186, adp images 193, Jasper Image 206; iStock: Empato 29, Peter Burnett 106, Brian Smith 133; Marc Millar Photography: 13, 14, 15, 40; Visit Scotland: photo Paul Tomkins, all rights reserved, 30

The photo on page 30 is from Glenfarclas

Illustrations by Heather Gatley [5, 7, 11, 22, 63]

About the Authors

Cameron Ewen

In 2013, The Balmoral, Scotland's most prestigious luxury hotel, brought to life its vision of opening SCOTCH, one of the best-stocked whisky spots in Scotland, now home to around 500 Scotch whiskies from distilleries old and new. Whisky Ambassador and bar manager Cameron Ewen brings both knowledge and passion to SCOTCH. Having joined the team in 2015, Cameron has spent time with a variety of whisky producers, further increasing his knowledge of Scotland's greatest export. His warm personality coupled with the relaxed ambience makes SCOTCH one of Edinburgh's must-visit bars.

Moa Reynolds

Moa is a whisky writer and spirits judge. Her writing appears primarily on Instagram and YouTube and in blogs, where she also collaborates with whisky brands from all over the world. She has contributed to publications such as *The Whiskey Wash*, *Whisky Magazine*, *Allt Om Whisky* and The Scotch Malt Whisky Society's *Unfiltered*. She won the Icons of Whisky Scotland (IWSC) Communicator of the Year 2021 and was shortlisted for the IWSC Spirits Communicator Award 2022.